The Little Book of Watercolor SECRETS

The Little Book of Watercolor SECRETS

A World of Practical Art in Your Pocket

Jacky Pearson

DAVID & CHARLES
— PUBLISHING —

www.davidandcharles.com

Contents

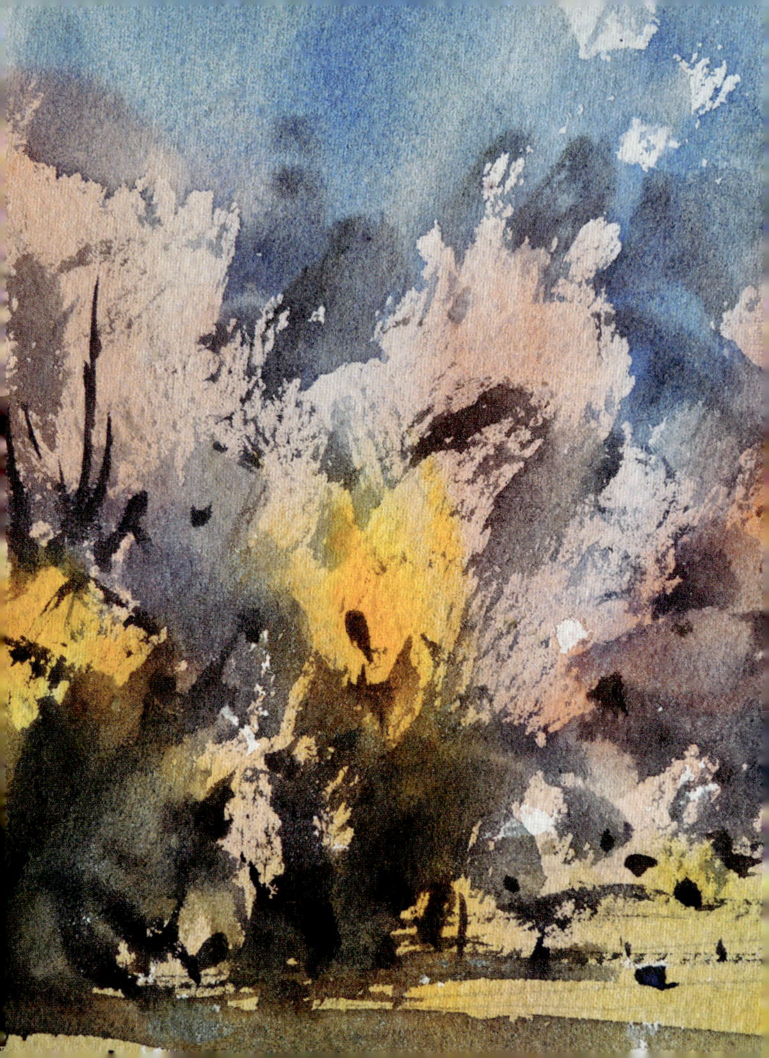

Introduction

What makes us fill a blank sheet of paper or a canvas with colors and marks? I have often pondered this but, whatever the answer, it is a primeval urge to be creative which is deeply engaging on an emotional level. Of all the mediums, watercolor is my passion! It can be my best friend when it goes well or my worst enemy when things don't turn out as I'd hoped. It is not for the faint-hearted but it is so rewarding. Just the beautiful transparency and perfect clean glow that can be achieved is something that continues to inspire me.

This quick sketch on an early morning outing, on the shores of Wellington Harbour, always brings back lovely memories of stillness: just me, and the birds, and calm water.

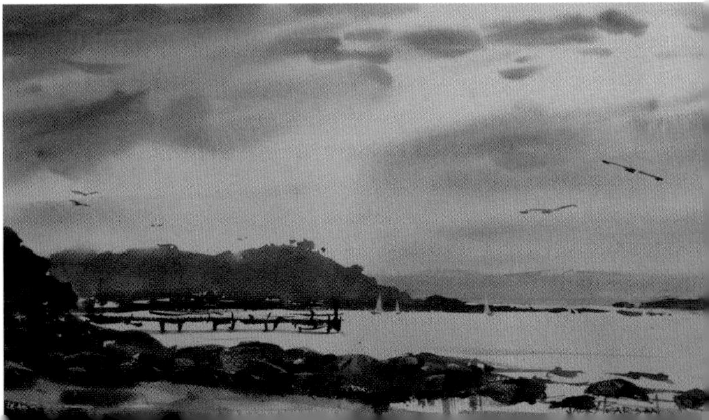

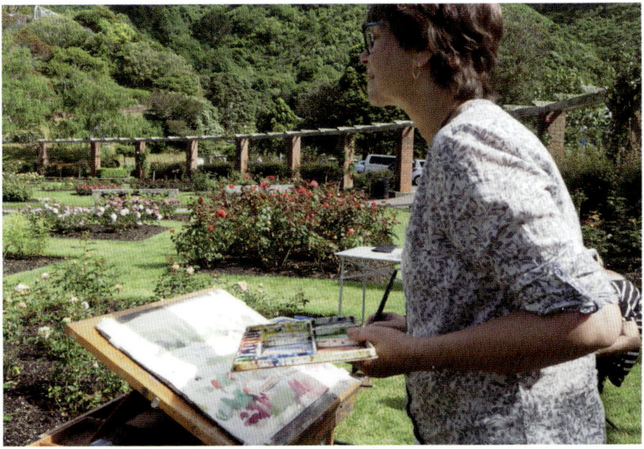

My style is direct realism, painting on location or in the studio. I try to paint a feeling, and paint to study light and shadow in nature. Although I paint in other mediums, such as oils and charcoal, it is watercolor that particularly makes me happy.

In this book, I hope to instill not only my passion for the medium but some short cuts that I wish I had known years ago when I was beginner.

CHAPTER 1

Essential Materials

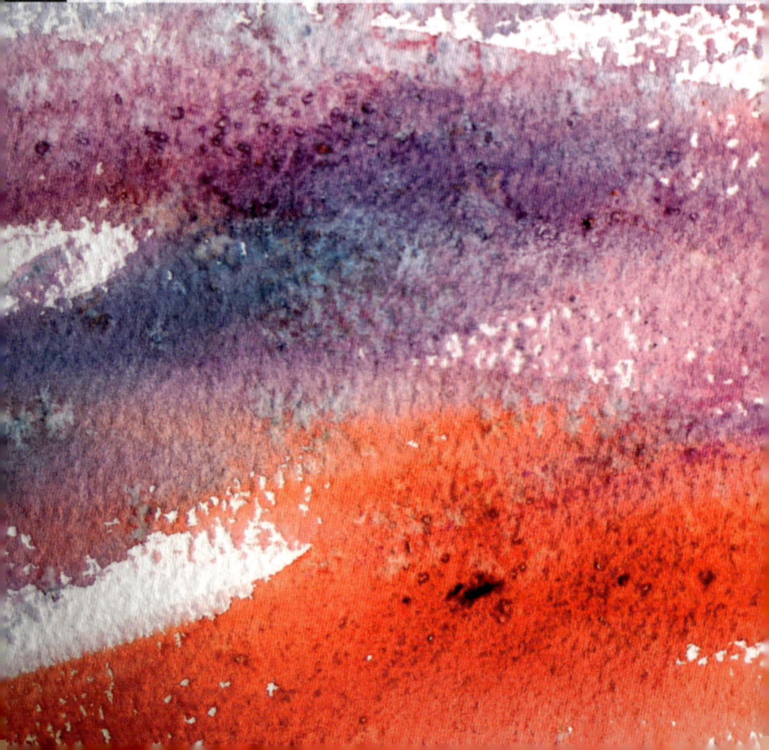

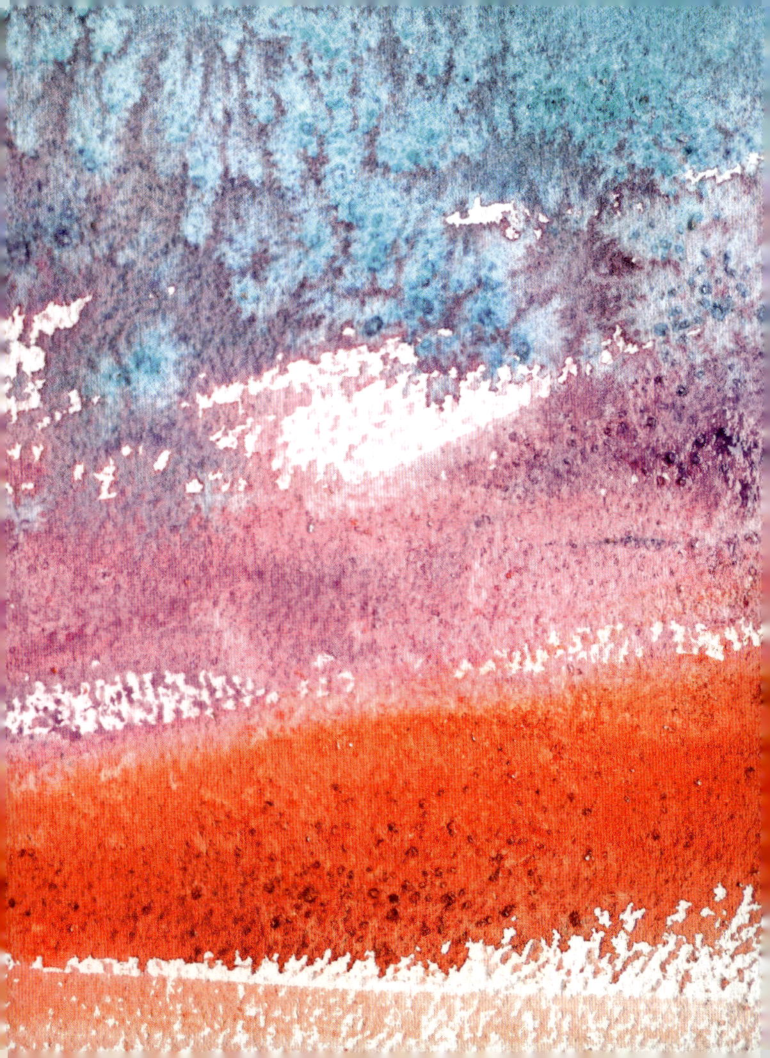

An Artist's Toolkit

This chapter focuses on selecting and understanding the materials that you need to begin your watercolor painting practice. There is one main point to remember, and that is you don't need a lot of equipment. Keep it simple!

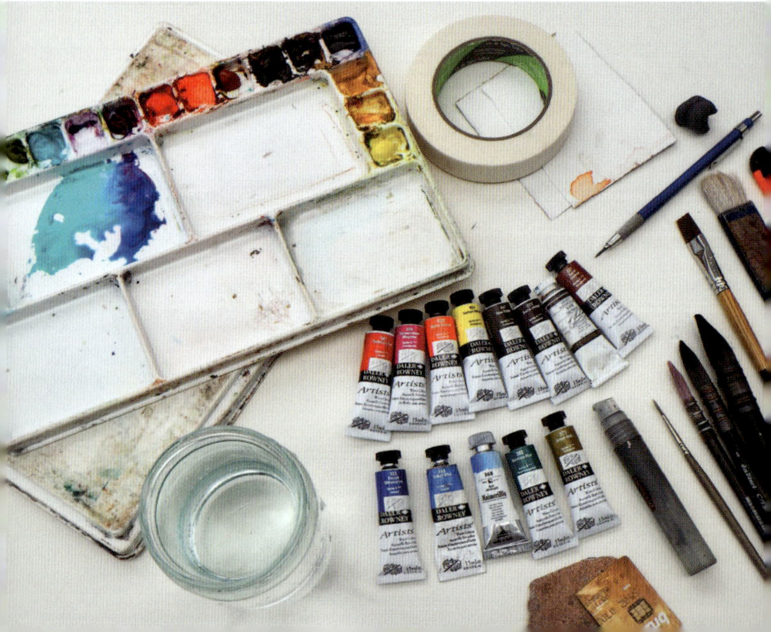

Setup

Timing is crucial to the painting process and any distractions need to be reduced (see Timing in Chapter 4 for more details). Cut time looking for or reaching for equipment by making sure you are set up and ready to go before you begin.

- Make your setup as efficient as possible, with everything in easy reach.
- Have your jar of water full so you don't have to keep checking where the water level is.
- Have your palette and jar of water on the side you hold your brush so you don't reach across the painting.
- Don't cram all your brushes into your water jar while you're working. You'll struggle to find the right one and slow the pace you can work at.
- Tape your paper down so water doesn't seep under and return as a runback (see Chapter 4).
- Keep your art board free of any clutter so you can tip your board quickly and easily.
- Have a pencil handy throughout the painting process so you can make some light marks on the paper to figure out a shape.
- Choose the brushes you need and have them separated from the others to save time, and have the paint you need squeezed out.

Watercolor Paper

Paper has the biggest impact on your painting, so choose carefully. There is an array of papers on the market, so try out as many as you can because they all give a different look to a painting. However, don't use paper that's more than two years old. The surface of the paper can break down, making it more like blotting paper and causing brown marks.

BUYING PAPER

You can buy paper as loose sheets, pads, gummed blocks, and rolls. Go for 140lbs (300gsm), or heavier, as it will cope with the amount of water applied to it without warping. I use a minimum of 140lbs (300gsm) for all my paintings.

There are two standards of paper for sale: artist quality and student quality. Artist-quality paper uses 100 percent cotton, is more expensive but tougher for certain techniques. It is acid free for longevity, and it won't fox (the term used for brown spots that appear due to aging).

Student-quality paper is good if you're on a tighter budget. Be aware that there are some so-called student's papers that are horrible to work on and won't give you clean washes. Experiment with different types, as it may not be you—it might be the paper!

GRADES OF PAPER

There are three grades within these two standards.

1. Rough: suits broad, loose washes, stays wet longer, and helps granulation (see Chapter 7), but fine detail is more difficult to achieve.

2. Cold pressed: also known as NOT ("not hot pressed") or medium. This is a good average paper, although runbacks can occur more easily. Student-quality cold pressed paper isn't great so use the student-rough version instead.

3. Hot pressed: also known as smooth. This suits fine detail and wet-on-dry techniques. Runbacks can happen (see Chapter 4), but little granulation can occur (see Chapter 7).

THE IMPORTANCE OF "TOOTH"

Watercolor paper has a texture known as a "tooth." This is the dimple on the paper that dictates how paint sinks or floats. You will find a wide variety of interesting textures pressed into paper between and across brands. The paper grades outlined are based on the tooth of the paper.

GUMMED BLOCKS

Paper also comes in gummed blocks, which doubles up as an art board. Paint on the attached paper then slide a knife or credit card around the border to separate it. Look for a small area on the edge that is ungummed to start the removal.

This painting is on New Zealand flax paper, which gave it an unusual, lively texture. Any textured and sealed handmade paper would work with watercolor.

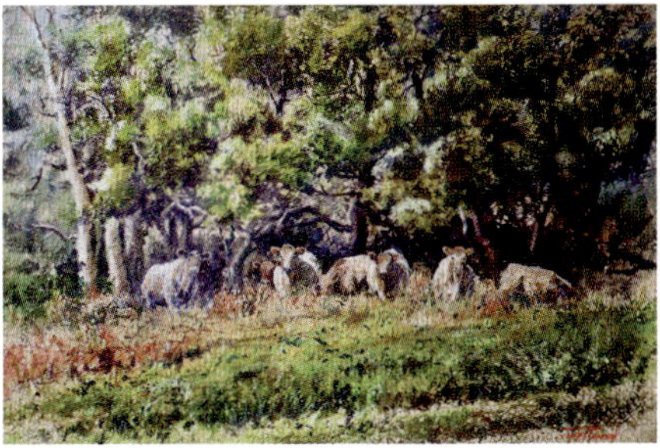

Paint

Watercolor paint is water-soluble transparent liquid in tubes, or hard blocks in pans. You can buy it as powder and make your own watercolor by mixing with gum Arabic and glycerin. It also comes as opaque paint known as gouache.

PAN PAINT OR TUBE PAINT

Both tube and pan paint start life as dry pigments that are ground up and mixed with binders such as gum Arabic, glycerin, or honey. The carrier in tube paint makes the paint soft and runny, whereas pan paints are compressed and dense. I use tube paints for my studio paintings. Half-pan paints are ideal for traveling and come with a built-in palette. However, pan paint does not allow a large amount of paint on your brush so it will have a smaller tonal range than tube paint and suits smaller paintings.

ARTIST OR STUDENT PAINTS

Artist paint is more expensive but is more concentrated, brighter, and comes with less filler. However, there are some excellent student paints available, such as Fine (Daler Rowney), Cotman's (Winsor and Newton), or Shinhan. Be aware that very cheap paint may contain so much filler that a tube runs out quickly.

GOUACHE

Gouache is opaque watercolor and used to create paintings with little or no white paper showing through the washes.

COLOR PALETTE

You won't need to buy a large number of paints to start with. My recommendation for a limited set of essential colors are Ultramarine Blue, Viridian Green, Burnt Sienna, Quinacridone Magenta, Cadmium Red, Raw Sienna, and Lemon Yellow.

If you choose to add to your palette, consider buying Cobalt Blue, Pale Turquoise PG50, Ultramarine Violet, Raw Umber, Burnt Umber, Pyrrol Orange, Indian Yellow, and White gouache (Titanium is the whitest).

I don't buy black, as it's too homogeneous. I mix my own from Ultramarine Blue, Quinacridone Magenta, and Burnt Sienna.

I use Quinacridone Magenta, but be aware that student brands don't make this. Look out for a cool red instead, like Alizarin Crimson. With artist brands, there are several Magentas that are all very similar, so you may find a different one works for you.

See Chapter 7, for more on paints and colors.

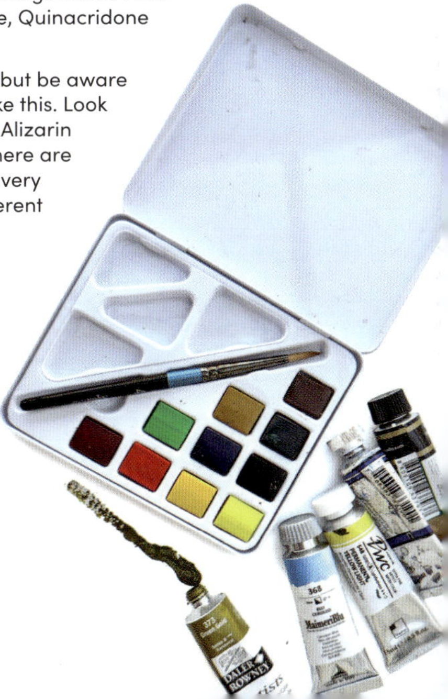

PIGMENTS

You can identify a color by its code, which is useful because your favorite color might have a different name across brands. You will find this information on the side or on the back of the paint label. One example is Daler Rowney's Warm Orange. It has many other names across different brands. However, they all use the same pigments code of PO73, which stands for Pigment, Orange, Hue 73.

Take note of the permanence rating (ASTM) of brands and if you are planning to sell your work, make choices of hues that are lightfast and not rated less than "durable." If you are a beginner or sketching, it would be fine to use "fugitive" colors.

Color names can be wildly different between brands, so get to know your paints. Here are three types of Cerulean Blue, and although they may not appear different, the variation will become apparent once you start painting!

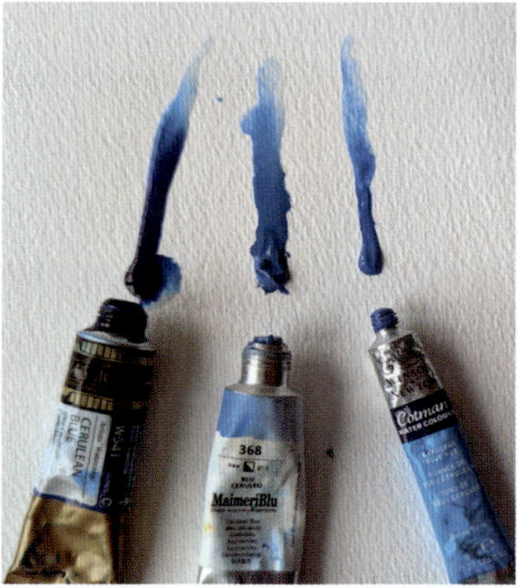

Brushes

There are many brushes on the market in all shapes and sizes, it's worth trying out as many as you can to see what suits you. To maintain your brushes, never leave them soaking in a jar of water or you might unglue some of the brush hairs. The brushes listed below are my "go-to" brushes.

1. Pointy wash brush, around the width of your thumb, for covering large areas of a painting. I also have a couple in bigger sizes.

2. Small synthetic pointy round brush, for smaller details.

3. Japanese 1in (2.5cm) Hake brush, for cutting in and for adding wet-on dry-glazes. I often use a large flat brush for these as well.

4. Small ⅜in (1cm) synthetic flat brush, for lifting wet and dry paint.

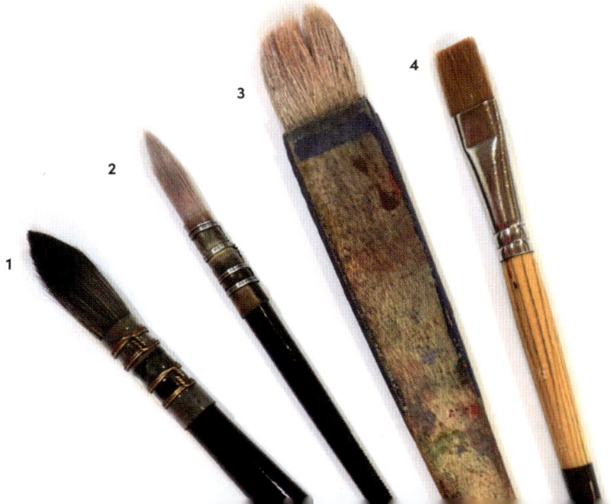

Palettes

Buy a large palette with a lid and deep, large mixing areas. If your paint dries up, rinse the palette under a tap to clean and soften the existing paint. Then squeeze new paint on top of the old, and the gum Arabic in the new paint will soften up the dried paint underneath.

Never squirt colors into the mixing areas! You'll lose control of the mixing process if you do this.

Split your colors into cools (blue, green, and violet) and warms (red, orange, yellows and earth colors) and arrange your palette into these two groups. If you're a beginner, try using a waterproof marker pen to write abbreviated names on the outside of the palette, such as UM for Ultramarine Blue, CR for Cadmium Red, RS for Raw Sienna, and so on.

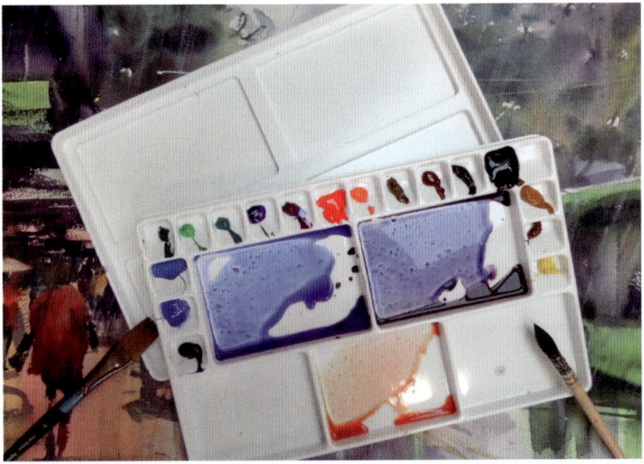

Other Tools

Masking tape: use buff-colored, medium-tack tape. Colored tape doesn't adhere well, and the color will affect your color perception as you paint!

Pencils: 2B to 4B are the most suitable grades to use on watercolor paper. If you use a harder pencil, you can damage the paper surface and a softer pencil might not erase.

Water jar: a large wide water jar filled to the brim. With a 1¾ pint (1 liter) full jar, I don't usually need to change my water during an average size painting. As you progress, the tonal values generally get darker, so clean water is not required.

Art board: Gatorfoam board, hardboard, or corflute. It should be large enough to allow you to comfortably tape your watercolor paper to it.

Painting angle prop: if you haven't got a desk easel, a short piece of wood gives you two angles for your board for gravity washes.

Chalk or white pastel: for adding some small highlights.

Tissues: these are much better for cleaning a palette than using paper towels.

Old towel: put a towel under your art board to catch the drips when painting at an angle, and use it to wipe your brushes.

Craft knife: for scraping through paint to reveal the white of the paper to create details, for instance, for glints on water.

Spray bottle: for making watery effects and altering edges on your painting as you go.

Old credit card: for scraping nearly dried washes to make hard edges for details.

CHAPTER 2

Find Your Subject

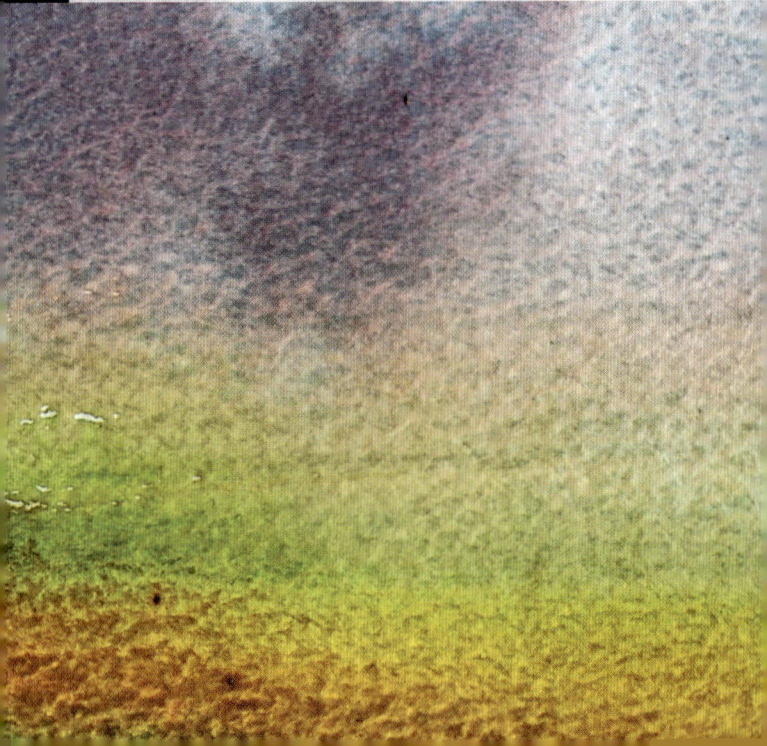

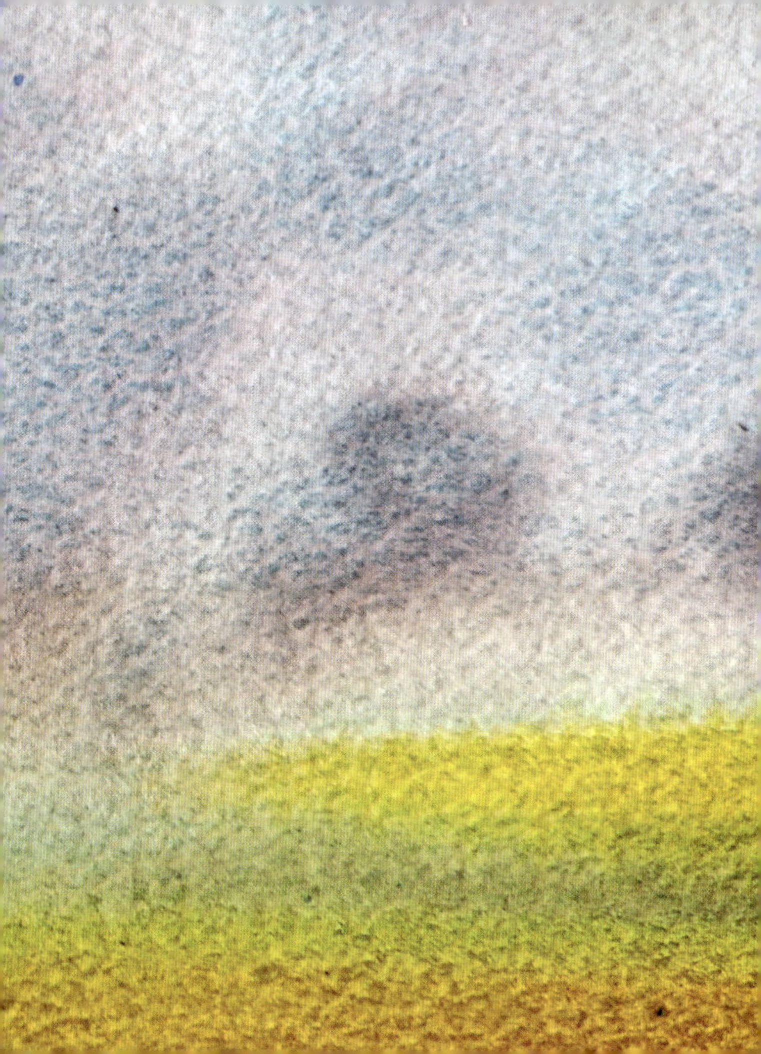

Choosing What to Paint

Choosing a subject is the first step in any painting process. This chapter gives you ideas to help you explore a wide range of subject possibilities. A scene experienced by you will have more emotional impact than using someone else's photograph. I make a point never to use anyone else's reference material. As much as possible, I paint on site, as this way I usually come across more than one subject option.

My Favorite Subjects

I look for subjects that allow me to use beautiful washes with smaller areas of finer detail. I have always been a romantic at heart and love nature, and want to capture its beauty. I love large areas of shadows. Atmospheric subjects include water, landscapes, and portraits. Strongly lit areas are always good because watercolor does darks really well due to the transparency of the medium, so it's great if you can master strong and transparent shadows.

My daughter, Alice, told me, "Mum, you've got to paint a feeling." My son, Niall told me to, "Avoid painting everything that's there." He said, "Focus on what is important and blur everything else." Wise words that I took to heart!

MY ADVICE

- Be open to different subject matter and look around your environment.
- Always carry a camera and a sketchbook.
- Choose a subject you know will show off what watercolor does best—depicting light due to its transparency, with beautiful passages of color.
- Any subject that you have a feeling about, or a connection with, is worth painting.
- Understand there are always things to learn on this creative journey.

I have always loved looking at the pattern of reflections on still water. "Reflections: Mangahao River" 2025, Langton Prestige rough.

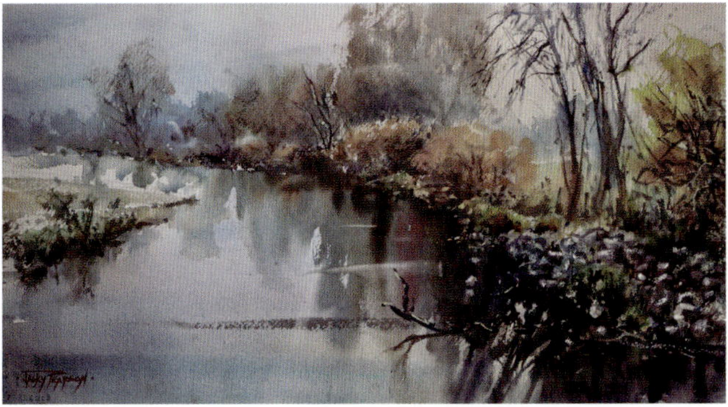

The Outdoors

I am always on the lookout for a new subject. A long car journey is ideal to observe a variety of clouds, fields, towns, rivers, and people. My husband is very patient.

"Stop!", I cry, having just spotted a new subject.

I have learned that, if I don't have much time on site, to at least walk around the subject because an even better aspect might be just a few steps away.

This painting was a result of a walk on Matiu-Somes Island in Wellington Harbour, New Zealand. The unusual slope of the ground with the wind-bent fir tree attracted my eye. The lovely colors of the grass on a hot day with strong, colorful shadows on the cooler side of the palette, provide the painting with a wonderful contrast.

"Grazing in Peace" 2019, Arches rough.

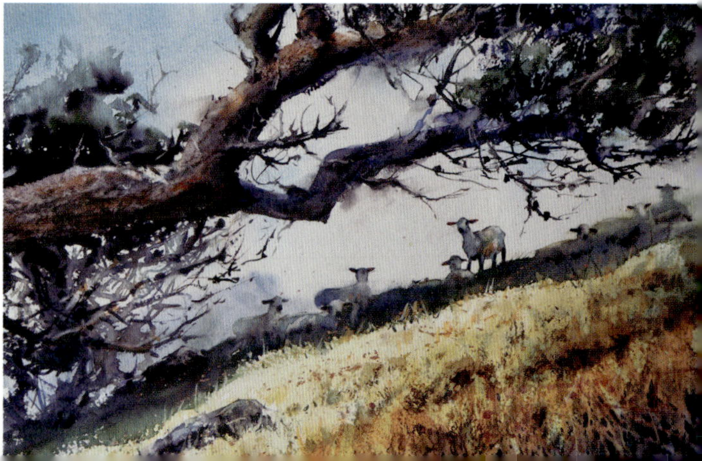

Painting From Photos

Not everyone can get out and about easily, however, one option is to use photos as a reference point. On those occasions where you do get outside, have your phone or camera at the ready. If you use other people's photos, seek permission and be aware of copyright laws.

Photographs can be easier to work from than real life but they do have their challenges. Here are some pitfalls to look out for, and how to avoid them.

1. If your photo has little life (no strong lights and darks), then imagine a different color or value set up and then paint that instead.

2. What works in a photo won't necessarily work in a painting. Be prepared to blur objects together, move objects, and crop the scene. Draw the eye to the focal point more than a photo by softening the surrounding area.

3. Photos will change linear and atmospheric perspective. Be aware hills will look flattened and in a portrait photo, hands or noses might appear nearer or bigger!

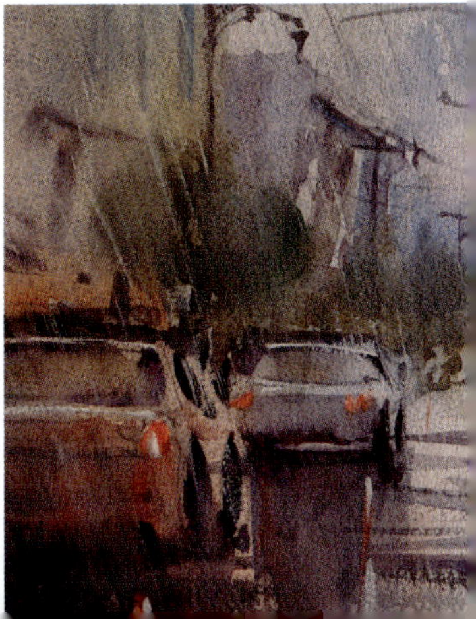

This rainy street scene was loosely derived from a photo I took in Wellington.

Light and Shadow

Painting nature is as much about understanding natural light as anything else. Study, as much as possible, the effects of natural light and shadow in real life, as this is the best tuition you can get. If you do this, ideas for painting subjects will pop up everywhere! Look out for a strong composition, with a good light and dark pattern.

Get into the habit of studying and making sketches on the spot. Make notes in sketchbooks, scribbling anything relevant. Take your time, if you can. I need two hours to do a couple of thumbnail sketches and the painting.

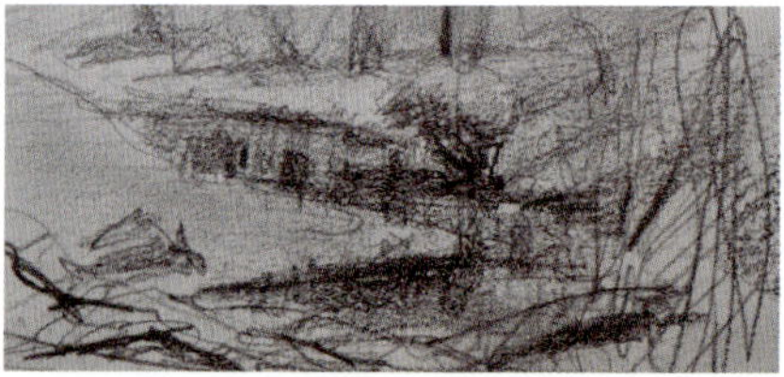

This outdoor sketch later became a draft for a more considered studio painting (see below).

"Crudine Valley Dry" 2019, Langton Prestige rough.

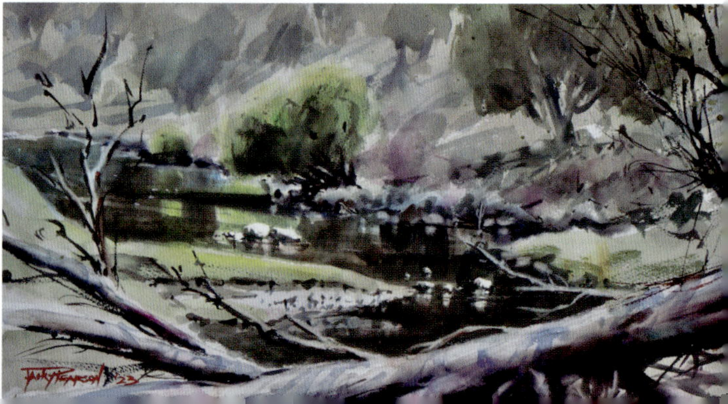

TIME OF DAY

The time of day that you decide to capture your subject will have an impact on what the light and the shadows are doing. The early morning, late afternoon, or evening is when the light is more atmospheric and shadows are long. If you like a particular subject matter, try painting it at different times of the day. I find that morning light appeals to me the most, with cool morning shadows and a feeling of getting the day going.

This was painted early in the morning, when the shadows had been deepened by the light on the water. I was so lucky to capture a boat as it rowed across the scene! "Morning at Chaffer's Marina" 2016, Arches rough.

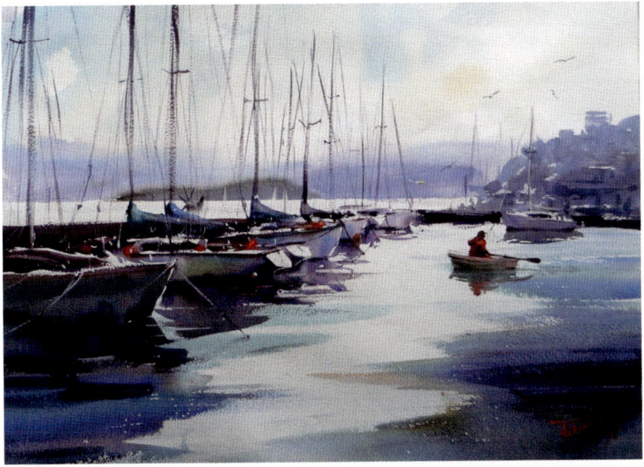

SHADOWS

Shadows are fabulous to paint. Rich darks are one of the hardest, but most important aspects, of a painting. If you look with a painterly eye, darks are never neutral or boring. They provide a perfect vehicle to show off beautiful color.

An old window in a woolshed made for an interesting subject because it features depth of shadows and lovely light effects on the glass. This forms a contrast with the peeling paint texture.

"Old Shed Window" 2020, Langton Prestige rough.

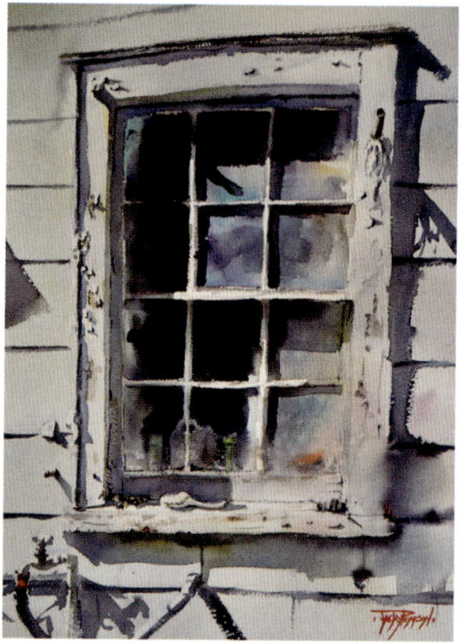

FLAT LIGHT

Despite what we have been discussing, flat light can make a good subject too. Usually, strong lighting makes a painting more striking but flat light (where there are no strong shadows) can be lovely with strong color or colorful washes as the dominant theme. Flat light can occur on gray, overcast days and doesn't cast much shadow.

Flat light can help boost colors like these autumn willows. Their color is brightened by being against a gray background. "Eely Point Autumn" Lake Wanaka, New Zealand, 2025, Langton Prestige rough.

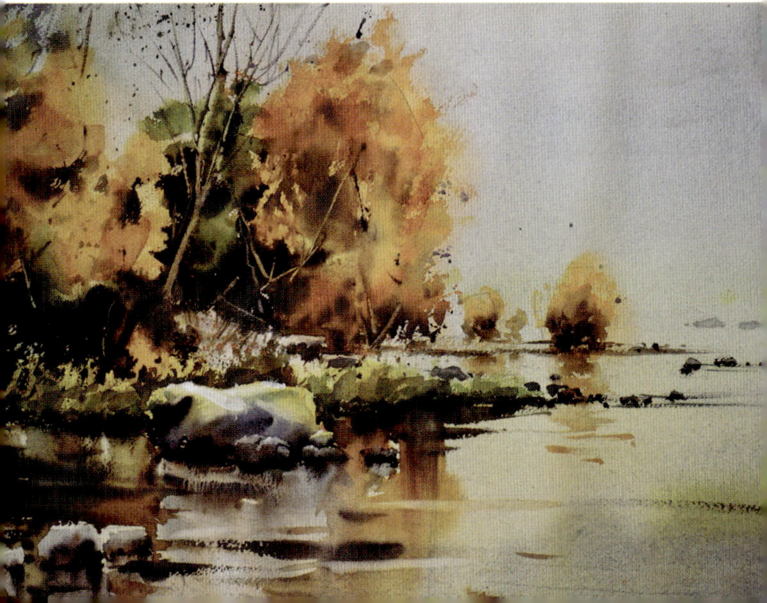

People

I am always interested in other people, capturing them in their everyday lives at work or relaxing. This human connection makes for a subject that has energy and a story. I have met some wonderful people by asking for their for permission to paint them.

Always ask permission from the person you are planning to paint. If you can't do this, or they say no, paint the person to look unrecognizable.

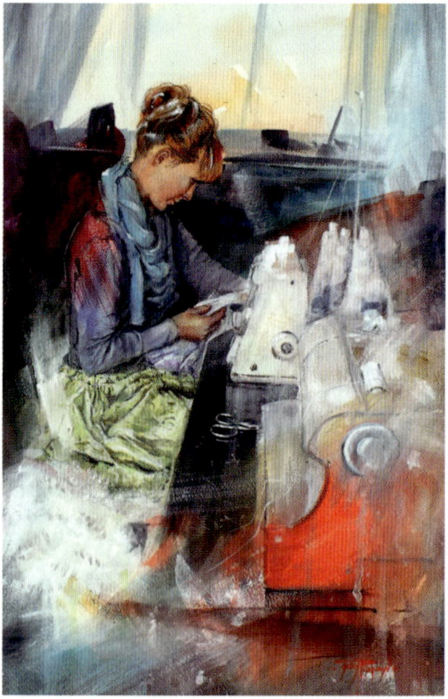

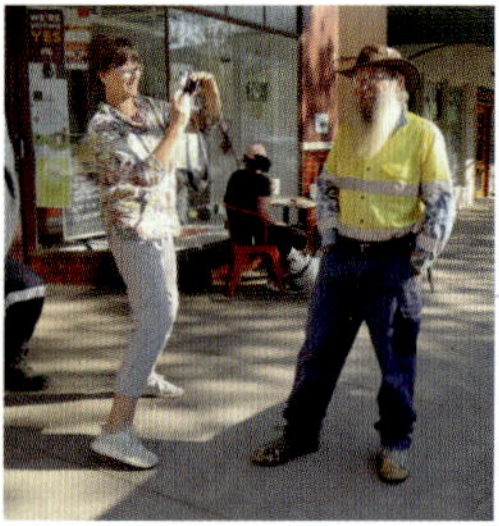

Be brave—they can always say no. I met Laurie in a coffee queue and I knew I had to ask him if I could paint him!

"The Seamstress" 2015, cold pressed illustration board.

"Laurie" 2024, Langton Prestige 100 percent cotton.

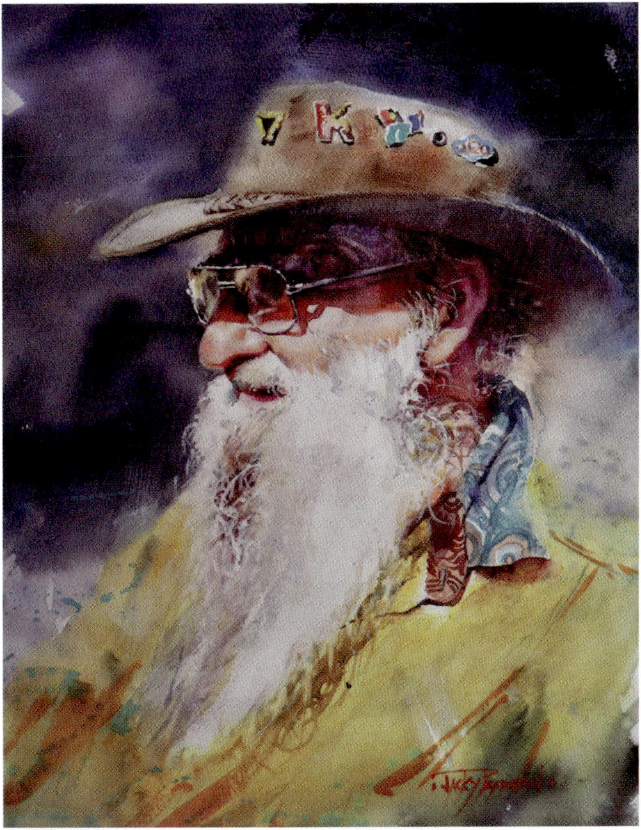

CHAPTER 3

Find Your Voice

Discovering Your Style

Your voice is a combination of your style and choice of subject matter. Your style will come out as you paint, just as your handwriting developed over time. My advice is to paint the way you love to paint, be passionate about what you do, and to follow your interests. This chapter has some helpful tips on developing your style and what you want to get out of being a painter.

A Starting Point

The wonderful thing about watercolor is that it's such an adaptive medium. The style options are limitless. Here are some practical ideas to help you get started.

- Paint what you love and love what you paint!
- Experiment with different types of brushes.
- Paint a picture in a set amount of time, in, say, 30 minutes. This is a very good challenge, and you might find you love the loose brush marks and freshness that results.
- Try a new color.
- Try out different papers.
- Paint with a friend at a set time every week.
- Make notes on what you love about other artworks and how you might be influenced by them but without copying.

- Interpret your photos by mixing a few together and moving elements, like trees, to make a more interesting composition.
- Paint to different kinds of music. Music has a huge bearing on our emotional interpretation of visual images.
- Get to know your subject better.
- Give yourself the goal of entering an exhibition.
- Do a series of tonal sketches and then paint a draft version using only three colors.
- Join an art group and meet like-minded people for ideas and encouragement.
- Develop your observational skills, noticing and recording as much as you can.

I have always loved the bustle of city streets, which is great to capture in watercolor and in a direct style, where broad strokes meet detail. "Wellington Summer" 2022, Arches rough.

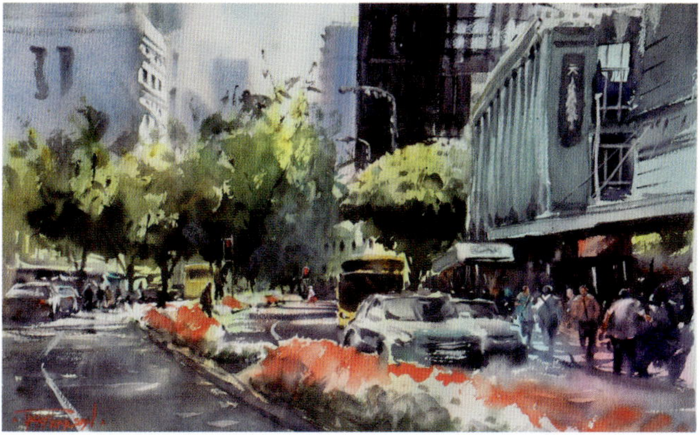

Influence

We are influenced by what we are exposed to. Our style preference is a blend of our personality and nurture. Once you have learned some techniques, study other artists' styles, make notes, visit galleries, and paint often. It is a love of the process that will help you develop a style. You will always be learning and adding to your repertoire. Enjoy the journey.

My strongest influence has been J.M.W. Turner (1775–1851). Each year, as a child, my mother Ann, took us to the art galleries in London. This had a profound influence on me wanting to paint. My favorites were always Turner's oils and watercolors, particularly the *Fighting Temeraire* and *Hero and Leander.* I was attracted by the super-charged atmospheric effects he managed to create.

Although this is a quick sketch painting, I have Turner's atmospheric effects in my mind. He did this by effortless merging of brushstrokes and color dramatics. "Wellington Harbour" 2023, Arches rough.

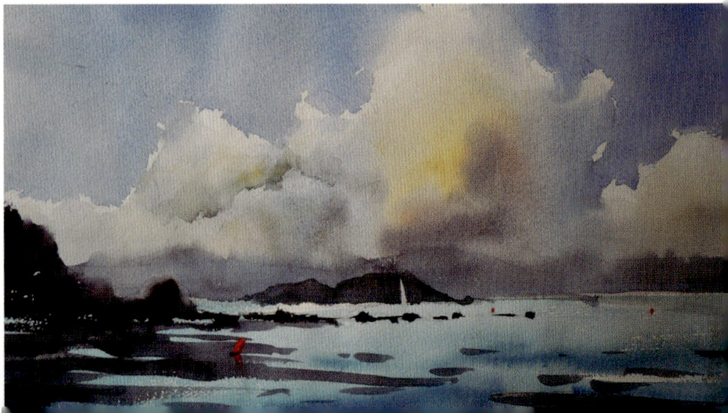

Inspiration

Inspiration can be instinctive and can be a fleeting feeling. My advice is to nurture your instincts, discover what you love, and what compels you to paint. I get very excited when I see a subject I just have to paint. I sometimes feel I am a journalist on the lookout for a good story! You might appreciate a particular style or artist, but you must enjoy the process of putting paint on paper.

I was constantly inspired, while living in Wellington, New Zealand, by the harbor and the city. I have always had a love of the water and where I lived, I saw the harbor every day. I have produced and sold countless paintings of boats sailing, marinas, and lighthouses. In Wellington, I found so much gorgeous architecture. Even when it rained, it was a wonderful opportunity to paint reflections on the roads and people rushing with umbrellas!

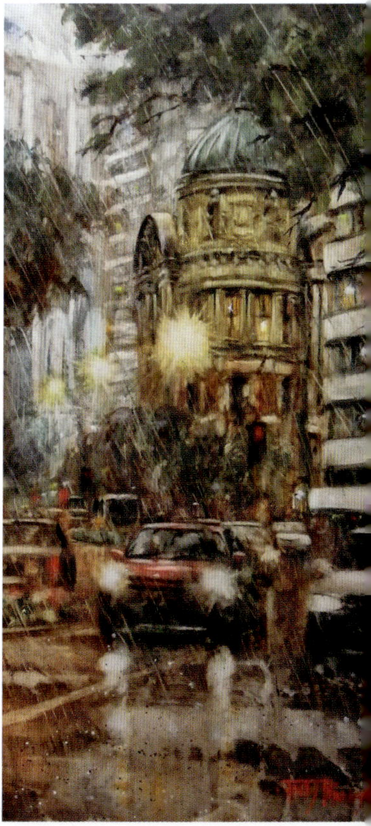

"Rain Again" 2015, illustration board.

Mixed Media

Anything goes. Watercolor lends itself to working with other mediums, such as combining watercolor with pastels wet-on-wet or wet-on-dry, or gouache, which is opaque and creates more solid color. Using different surfaces also makes a watercolor look very different. Although I am, mostly, a pure watercolorist, I do occasionally combine it with other mediums and have even used gold on hills to depict the Golden Hour when the sun was very low!

Finishing this painting of Rangitikei Gorge was fun! I added gold leaf to a few areas in the cliffs, I glazed several Cobalt Blue and Raw Sienna washes over the back of the river, and added some flicks and splatters in the foreground. "Rangitikei Gorge, Golden Hour" 2024, Khadi cotton rag.

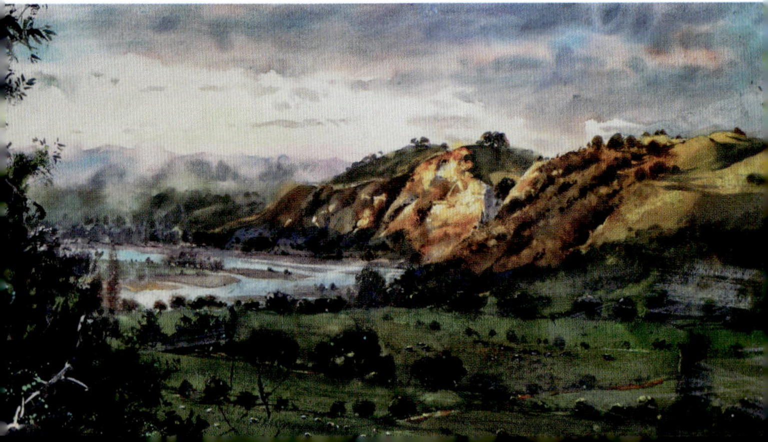

Embrace Color

My belief is that, rather than being a slave to color accuracy, go with your natural instincts for color. These instincts and preferences will form part of your style. Just make sure you use colors that go well together and try color swatches out on pieces of watercolor paper. Understand your color wheel and how colors work. Are you more inclined to cool or warm colors? I love turquoise. However, I am trying to paint with more warm colors and am appreciating a change in palette now and then. See Chapters 6 and 7 for more on color theory and color mixing.

The white horse was a base for the depiction of the warmth of the light. I wanted a softness of texture, and warm colors helped tell a story. "Old Friends" 2025, Indian Khadi rag paper rough.

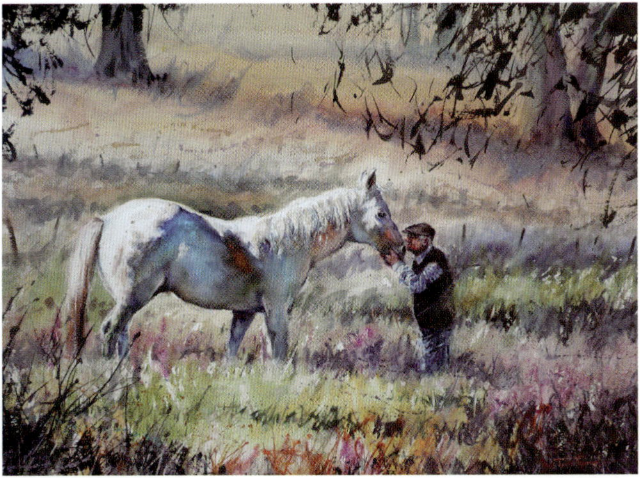

Realism

Your style will be greatly influenced by where you paint. From the quiet of your home to a busy street, both will affect how your brushstrokes are applied and the amount of time you spend developing washes and details. Realism, as a style, is about painting what you see and representing it in a realistic way. Working from photos at home will allow you the time to focus on small details and creating a painting that is true to life.

I don't often paint ultra realism, but I did to paint my husband Tony's hands. I used cold pressed illustration board that allowed me to add tiny delicate washes to build up layers and create the illusion of reality.

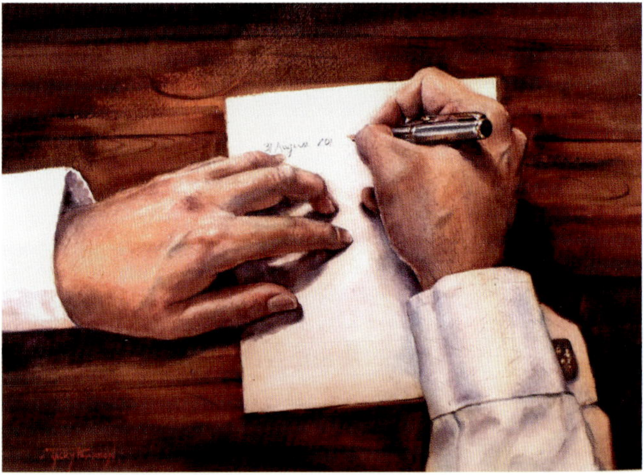

Years ago, I took my paintings into a gallery to see if they would take them. The experienced gallery owner pointed out I never put figures in. I felt my lack of expertise in figures would let my landscapes down. He suggested I go to life drawing classes and learn how to populate my paintings. I started going and got to really enjoy figures and portraits.

The whole exercise of drawing accurately trains your eye, brain, and hand coordination. This in turn helps your painting skills. It really sets you free to be imaginative.

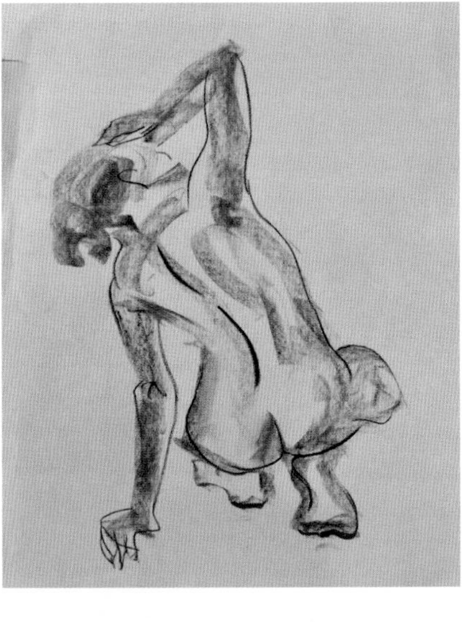

I created this sketch in life drawing classes in two minutes.

Get Out into Nature

Painting outdoors comes with a whole set of challenges. Outside, you are up against wind, tide, changing sun angle, people, and noise. These pale into insignificance when you "get the bug" and simply love the outdoor painting experience. Your style will probably be more direct with fewer brush marks. I tend to paint a draft outdoors and do it again as a studio piece. For me, it makes me feel alive and part of nature. I get so many ideas just being there. It has influenced my direct semi-impressionist style.

Have your sketch pad handy and camera at the ready for that fleeting "thing" that might happen! Low tide, morning, and early evening is always a great time to gather ideas and a feeling. You must have a personal connection so that you can put real feeling in a painting, it isn't just about good techniques.

This is an unpolished draft created on site of Matiu-Somes Island Lighthouse, overlooking Wellington Harbour. I was pleased at the way the lighthouse overlooks the city using value and pushing the blue in the distance.

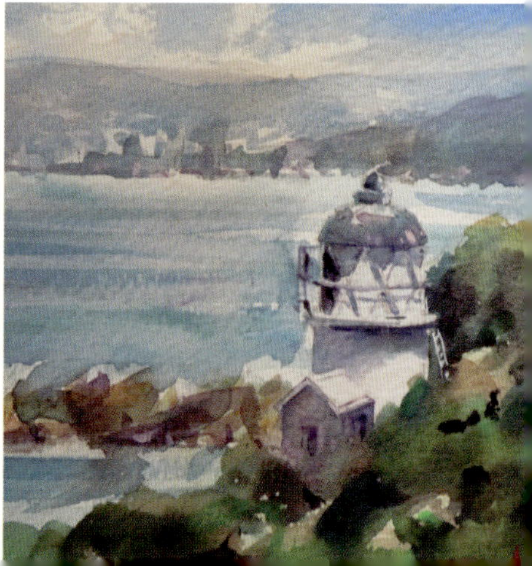

TRY THIS: KEEP EVERYTHING

Keep notes and sketches, and scribble ideas down. No matter how trivial, if you are drawn to them, they might spark an idea another time. Take lots of photos and categorize them in files. Blend photos together, change their color and tonal value, or move objects around if they aren't in a good position in the photo. Go on, move a tree! Around 80 percent of what you keep might never be used, but the 20 percent might inspire you.

I have so many photos of Wellington Harbour and have painted it so often, I can dream up sunsets and boat races. "From Worser Bay" 2024, Langton Prestige rough.

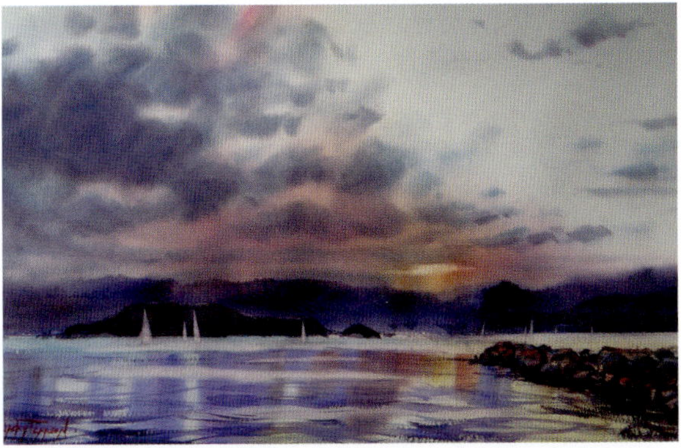

CHAPTER 4

Practical Techniques

Learning to Use Your Tools

Technique will set you free to paint in your own style. Watercolor painting is a relationship between water, pigment, gravity, and timing. The medium is alive when wet, and works best when it is running, and paint is mingling. This aspect makes it a very exacting medium and can be frustrating. Take your time, learn the techniques, and do not expect to fully control watercolor. Because watercolor is a transparent medium, it is generally best to paint from light to dark values. Then it's up to you to create and break the rules! Above all, enjoy the process. There is no such thing as a wrong way to paint, as long as the outcome pleases you.

The techniques in this chapter apply to tube paint as I like to achieve strong darks. If you use pan paint, they will require extra layering wet-on-dry to achieve the same strength of darks as tube paint.

Timing

In watercolor, timing is everything. You are trying to work before the water on your paper dries. Check on the wetness of the paper as you paint. Put your head level with the paper, positioned to the side, and look at the glisten. If it is very shiny, then it is at the soaking stage; shiny and it is at the wet stage.

You can carry on adding washes at these stages but if the shine is beginning to dull then either only add thick paint to get soft details, or to add further washes, let the paper dry before continuing. If your paper is drying too fast, use a small spray bottle to atomize the air over your work to keep it moist. We will look at timing and water again in The 1, 2, 3 Method later on in this chapter.

Working with Your Paper

You can either tape your dry paper onto your board with masking tape, or wet the back of your paper. This will keep the paper flat. The advantage of wetting the back is the paper will stay damp for longer and allow some nice paint developments in slower time. To keep the back of the paper damp for longer, you can lay it on a wet cloth.

Gravity will also play a role in your painting. Think of it as the speed of your paint. I move my paper on the board around to get an even look and control where the paint needs to go (see Types of Washes for more details).

Learn to paint in monotone to figure out values. It's very satisfying when you don't have to worry about finding a color.

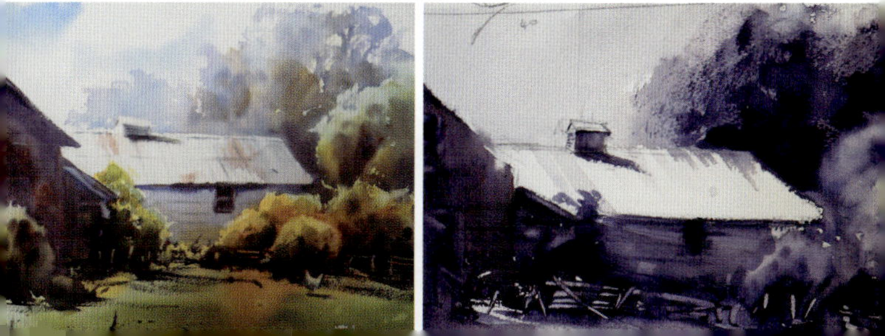

Brush Handling

The way a brush is held has a huge impact on paint effects. I usually stand to paint so I have a free arm, allowing me to use my whole arm, from my shoulder to my elbow with a flexible wrist. Hold your brush in three places: the middle of the stem, at the end, or near to the ferrule. You can have the brush upright at 90 degrees, 45 degrees, and almost parallel to the paper.

1. To hold your wash brush, hold the stem at about 45 degrees. Lightly grip with just your thumb and forefinger. The middle finger is the brush guide, the little finger is for balance.

2. Now turn your hand over to paint. Press lightly.

3. To scumble and make strong marks, hold your brush upright and at the top. Now put pressure on the stroke to rub the paint into the tooth of the paper.

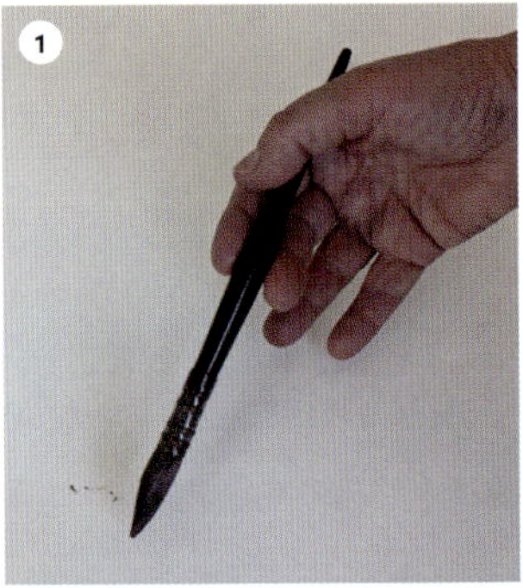

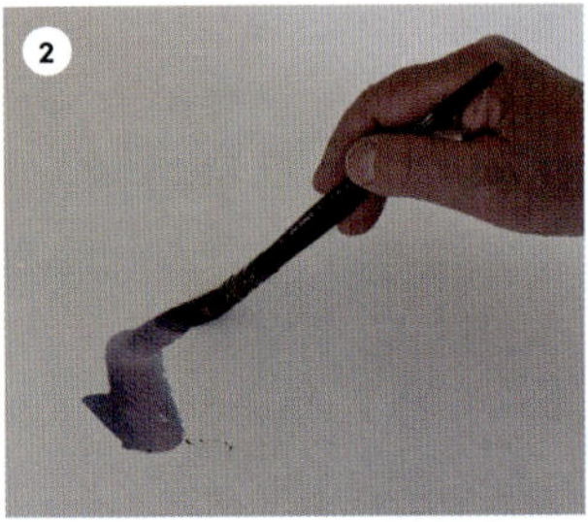

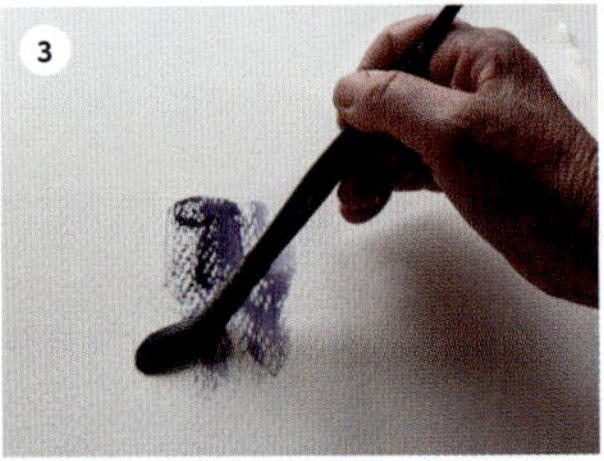

CHARGE YOUR BRUSH

Charging means loading your brush with paint. Watercolor looks lighter when it is dry, therefore the most beneficial brush technique is to load the brush with plenty of pigment.

THE BEAD METHOD

Knowing how to make a paint and water "bead" is essential for creating beautiful clean washes. It will form part of the next brushful of paint. After applying a runny mix of paint and water, tilt your paper on the board slightly to keep the paint moving. A bead of wet paint will form and acts as a reservoir. Load your brush with more of the same mix then go into the bead and push the wash along. Continue to create beads with each stroke, keeping the whole wash damp by regularly loading your brush. When finished, lay the paper flat and suck up remaining beads with the tip of a damp brush.

A bead has formed here at the bottom of the orange paint.

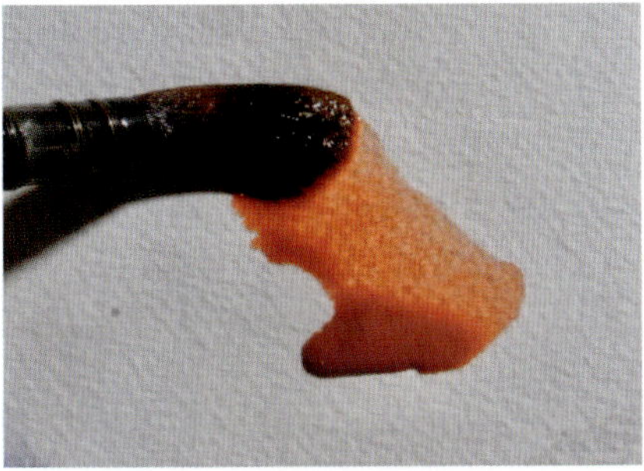

The 1, 2, 3 Method

In the palette, I've created three standard mixes of paint and water to help you understand what it is you are trying to achieve. You'll see No. 1, No. 2, and No. 3 mixes referred to throughout the book.

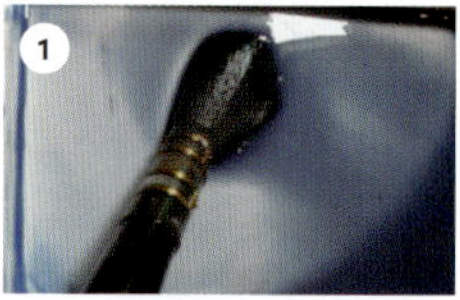

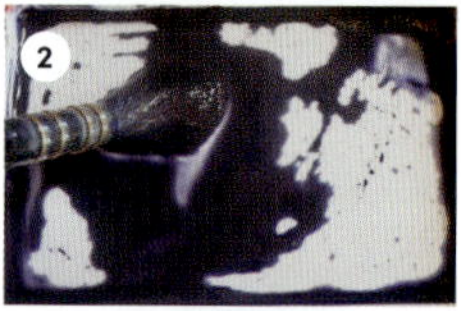

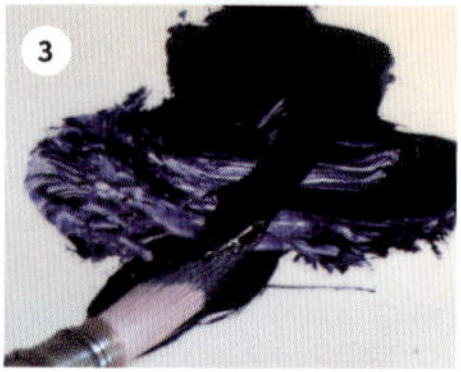

Watercolor painting generally requires establishing the light value washes first followed by darker values.

Mix 1: thin paint for washes, glazing, and the underpainting, giving a lovely moody start to a painting. Use lots of water and not much pigment.

Mix 2: medium paint for the middle stage and massing shapes. Use less water and plenty of pigment. It should move easily with the brush but not when tilting the palette.

Mix 3: the thickest paint is reserved for soft- or hard-edge details. Use only pigment, no additional water, and a damp brush.

Practice making as many variations as you can. Start with thin washes and add increasing amounts of paint to the mix: the more pigment, the thicker the paint, and the darker the tonal value.

You can also make "in-between" mixes, such as 1.5 or 1.75. Think of pigment as cornstarch in a sauce! Try out different mixes at different drying stages. Refer to Timing earlier in the chapter to understand wetness of paper.

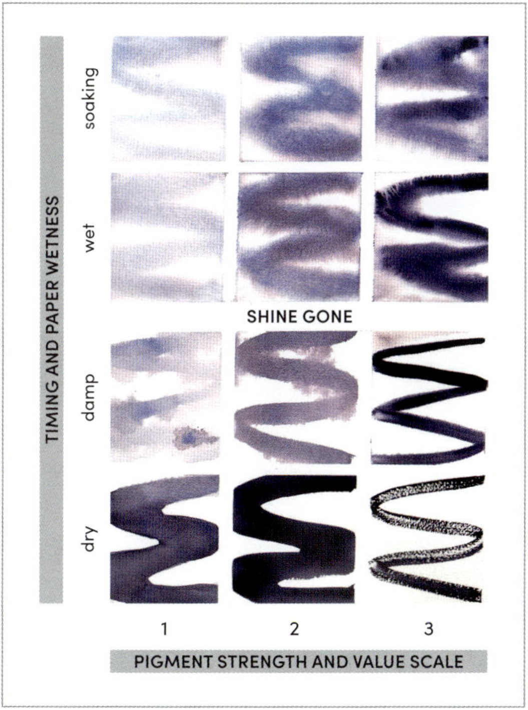

This table will help you understand the water–paint relationship, including what edges look like, and the tonal value effect from wet to dry paper.

Types of Washes

A wash is simply a mix of water and paint. I use plenty of water, have a fully loaded brush, and importantly, use gravity to control the paint on the paper for most washes. Have your board and paper at the angle that will achieve the look you want. If your paper is horizontal, there's no movement in the paint. More upright and it will pour down, and on a slight angle, the wash moves slower.

FLAT WASH

Keep the paper flat to keep the wash even. The paint is evenly distributed throughout the wash. Apply paint with a large brush with No. 1.5 mix. You may have to move your board slightly to distribute the pigment evenly. You can leave it to dry on a flat surface. Uses: glazing.

GRADED WASH

Have your board on a slight gradient of about 15 degrees. Load your brush with No. 2 mix, not too runny. Apply and make a bead form with gravity. Next, pick up the same No. 2 wash and dilute it by dipping your brush in the water (making a No. 1.5 mix) and brush this into the bead. Repeat this, making your paint thinner each time. Finish with clear water on your brush. Uses: sky or water.

VARIEGATED WASH

Mix the different colors you want to use on your palette in separate places. Use No. 1.5 mix so the wash is quite runny. Place them on the paper so each color drifts into the other, and use gravity, by tilting the paper to make the colors run where you want them to. Uses: underpaintings and sunsets.

For a flat wash, the color is applied evenly.

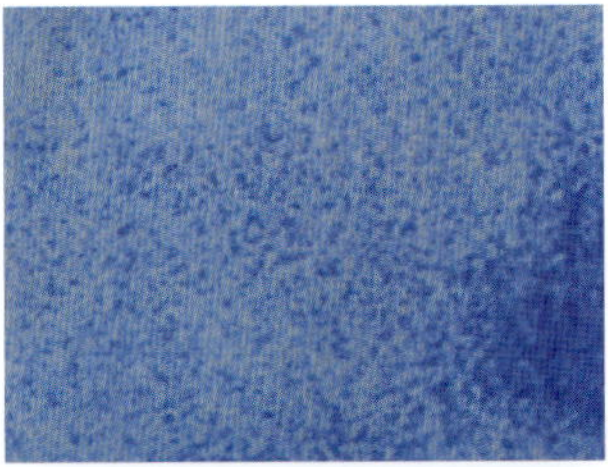

For a graded wash, keep the bead going to the bottom.

For a variegated wash, allow colors to mingle side by side.

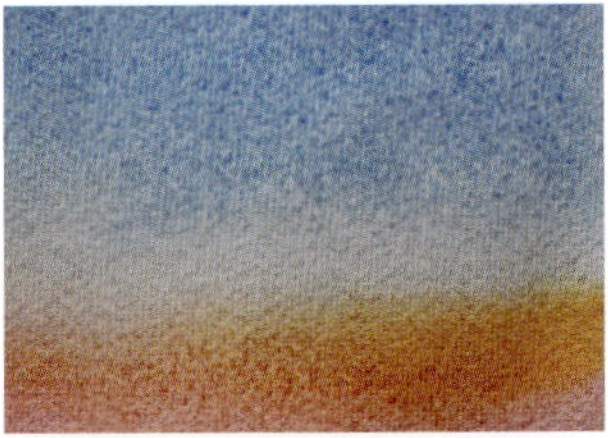

Dark Washes

To make darks, you need to not only choose a dark color such as Ultramarine Blue or Burnt Sienna but also use less water. To darken a wash, use less water and more pigment. To lighten a wash, then use more water and less pigment. Refer back to The 1, 2, 3 Method, as needed.

TRY THIS: THICKER IS DARKER

1. Using a pointy wash brush on dry paper, paint a simple boat (or square) with No. 1 wash of black. Have a slight tilt to your paper so a bead forms at the bottom.

2. Next, thicken the mix up with pigment (No. 2 mix), and without leaving a gap, go into the bead and make a darker mirror image.

3. On a dry area of your palette, thicken the mix again with the same dark pigment so it's as thick as possible (No. 3 mix). While both shapes are still wet, use a damp synthetic pointy brush and paint a dark, thick line between the two areas of wet paint.

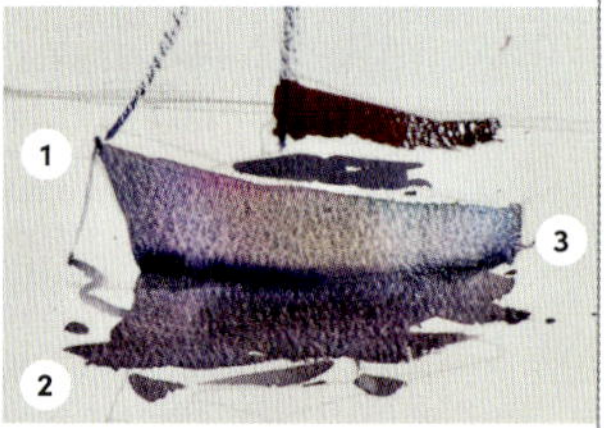

Play with the order of the washes by starting with very thick dark paint (No. 2 and 3 mix) and then adding No. 1 mix to see what you can create. This works well for tree trunks for instance.

Types of Edges

There are several types of edges in watercolor, all creating different effects. The wetness of the paper will determine the type of edge. You can rewet your paper at any stage during the painting process, or dry it in the sun or use a hairdryer. Edges are a powerful way of creating both movement and emotion.

Two key techniques to mastering edges are wet-on-dry (adding paint onto dry paper) and wet-on-wet (adding paint onto wet paper).

1. Wet-on-dry creates a hard edge. Use where edges need to be controlled.

2. Wet-on-wet creates a blurred edge. Drop paint into wet or damp paper. It will spread outwards creating lovely random effects. Use it to create a rounded form.

3. Both wet-on-wet and wet-on-dry together will create a variegated edge, useful for clouds and foliage. It can be created by dropping water before or after the paint is applied.

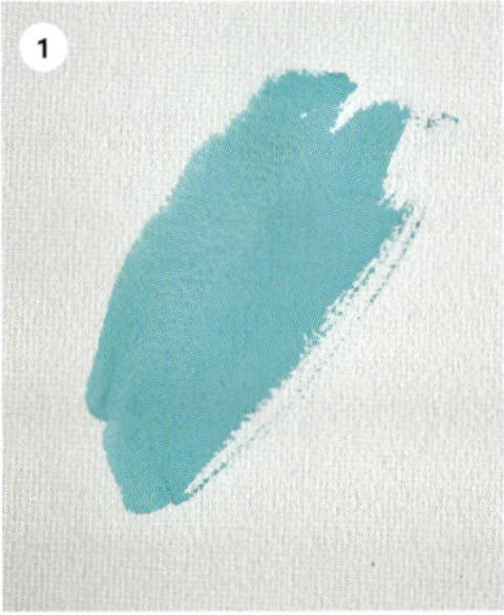

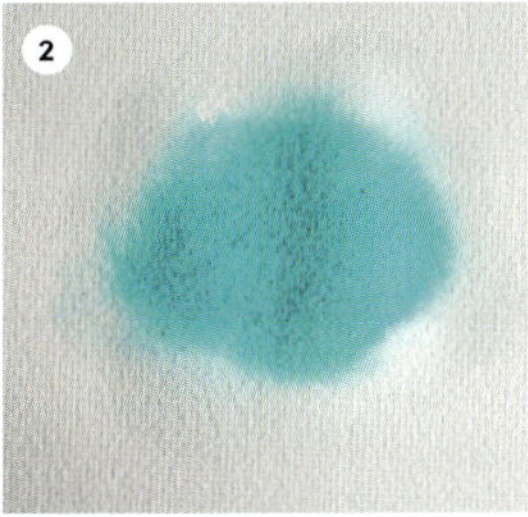

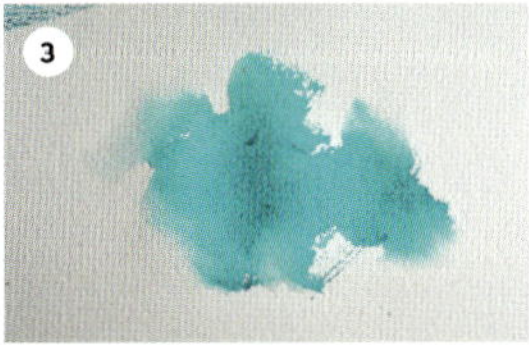

4. A quick dry brushstroke skimmed over rough paper creates a more scattered effect. This can denote movement, such as wind across the water.

5. Feathering creates a controlled softening of an edge. Apply a flat wash, wet-on-dry, with a flat brush. Immediately, apply clean water to the paper slightly away from the colored edge. Wiggle your brush towards the color and this will soften the edge. Use gravity by tilting the board to suit the edge you want.

6. Runbacks (or cauliflowers) happen when adding very wet paint to nearly dry paint. They can be used to create a specific effect but they can spoil a painting, so be sure to get your timing right.

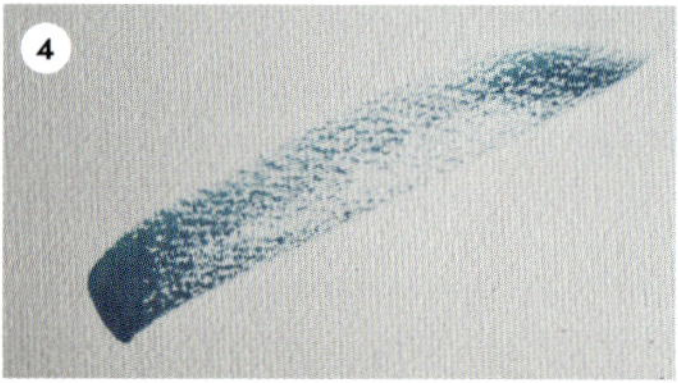

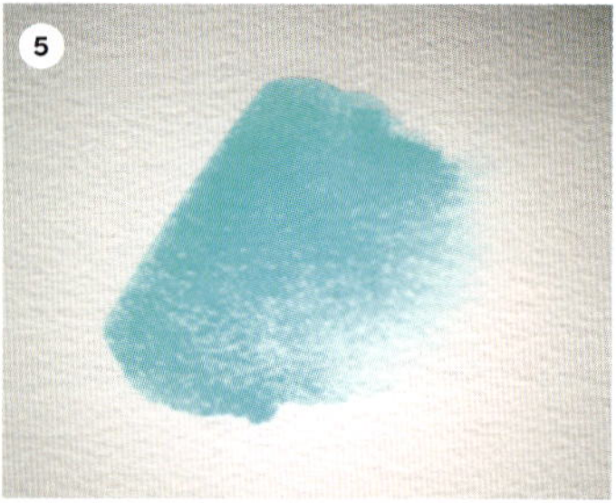

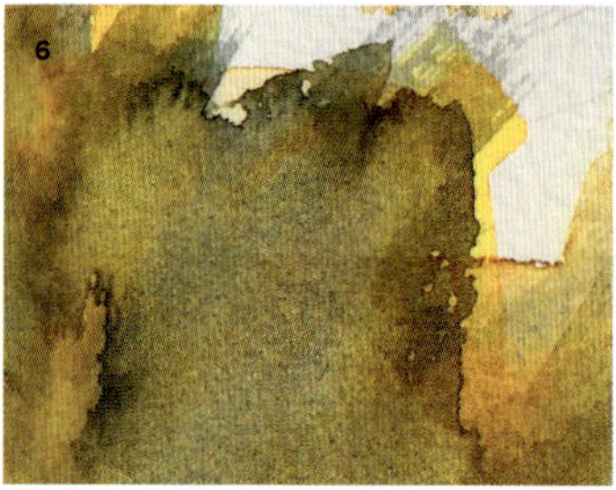

Glazing

Glazes are thin washes (No. 1 mix) of different colors laid on top of each other wet-on-dry or wet-on-wet. They are very transparent, allowing the paper and previous washes to show through. They help develop an area of atmosphere, changing tonal value or hue. A painting can have both wet-on-wet and wet-on-dry glazing, but remember, it's the last color that makes the overall difference. Use a wide flat brush for glazing.

1. **Wet-on-wet glaze:** lay down different-colored washes, one on top of the other, not waiting for them to dry.

2. **Wet-on-dry glaze:** lay down several thin washes one at a time, drying in between each one. This method gives a beautiful, delicate glow.

On this painting, I have glazed up to 10 thin wet-on-dry washes of white gouache, mixed to a thin milk consistency, dried in between Raw Sienna and Quinacridone Magenta washes to push the hill back.

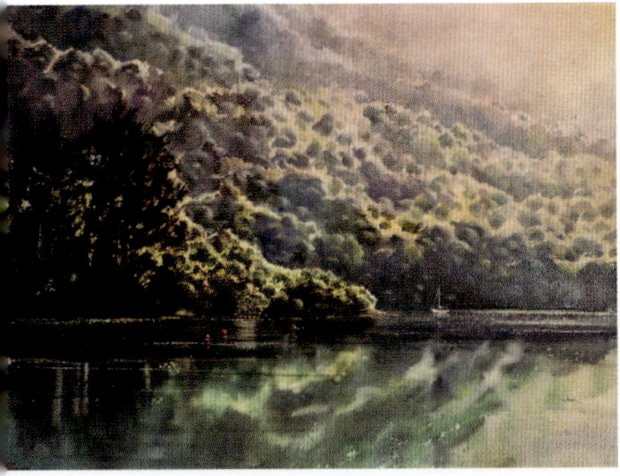

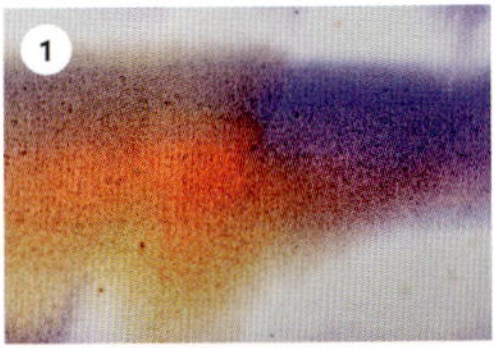

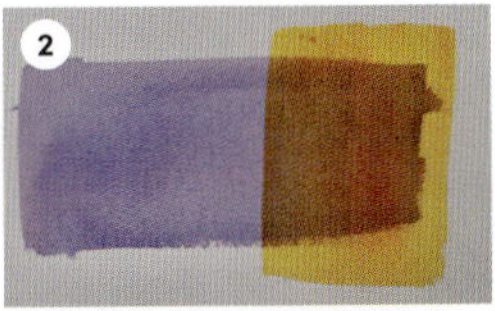

Preserving White Space

This is one of the most important skills to master in watercolor. The white of the paper is your light source for the painting—it glows through the paint—and is also your lightest value. It is important to leave white paper for large areas rather than adding white paint, which looks out of place with transparent watercolors. I use a large synthetic flat brush or a large pointy wash brush to "cut in" around the white space I want to keep.

Another option for this is to use masking fluid or tape, which allows you to paint over the area you want left as white paper and then remove the masking fluid when you are finished. However, it is quite difficult to make this look natural, and can look disjointed compared to the brushwork.

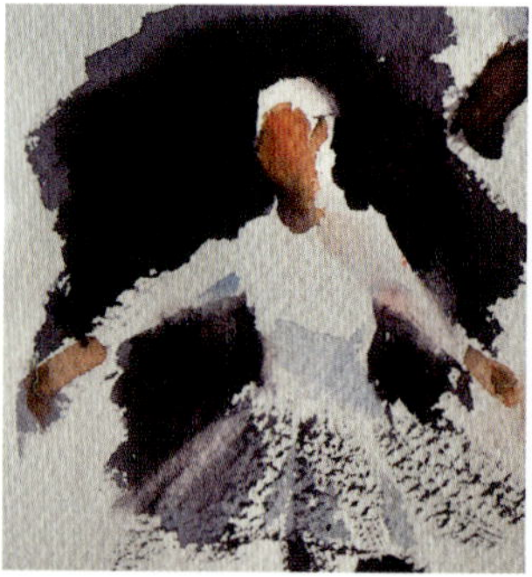

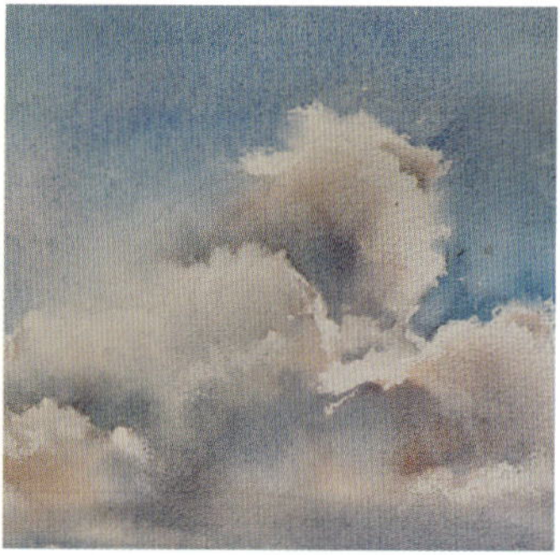

From figures to skies, preserving white space is an important technique to learn. White space will create a punchy liveliness to your painting.

Lifting

Often, you will need to redefine white areas that have been painted over. At the end of a painting, I spend a lot of time removing paint to create highlights. Using a clean, damp, flat synthetic (stiff) brush, gently rub the paint you want removed. For a more stubborn paint, clean your brush and repeat a few times. You can lift the paint when the paper is damp for a soft edge or when dry for a more defined hard edge.

Create Form

All the techniques in this chapter will help you create form in your painting, such as in this curl of hair. It was created by lifting, glazing, and feathering the hard edges of the glazes. There might be 10 thin glazes, all wet-on-dry, either side of the high point of the curl. The glazes were feathered and dried before applying each layer.

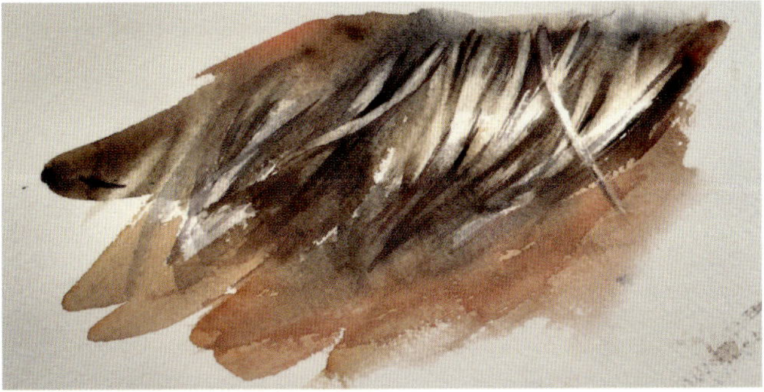

This is a practice hair curl from a portrait.

CHAPTER 5

Understanding Composition

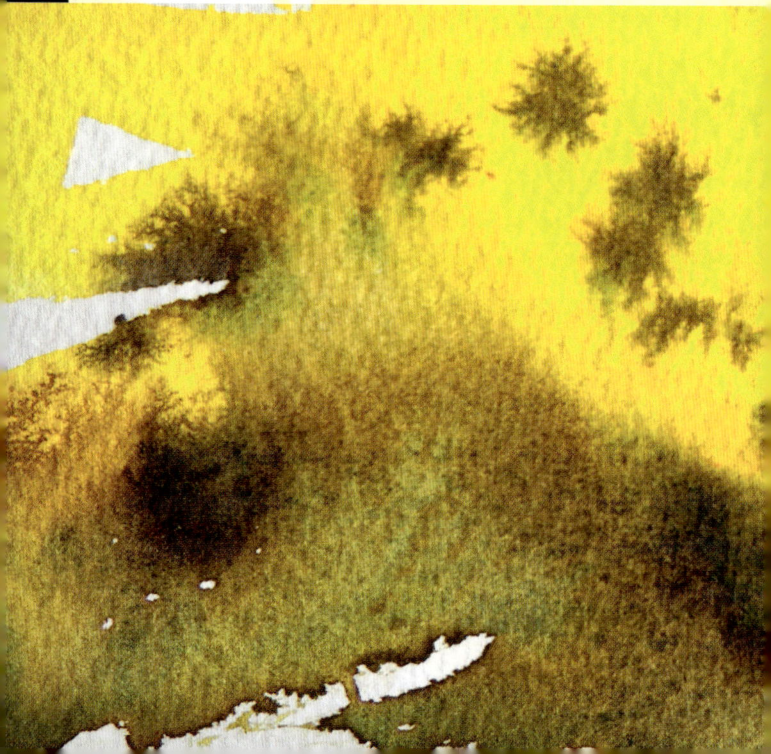

Arranging Your Artwork

My belief is that art is both an idea and technical skill brought together. Arguably, without a good composition, there is no artwork, no matter how technically good it is. If you liken painting to music, you are the conductor, the player, and the composer! Like music, a painting can provoke a powerful emotional response, but how to get that across is all in the composition. It is the "tune" of a painting.

I tried an unusual composition here, cropping to the right of the farmer's head, enabling me to more easily direct the eye to his features under the hat. "Farmer" 2023, Langton Prestige rough.

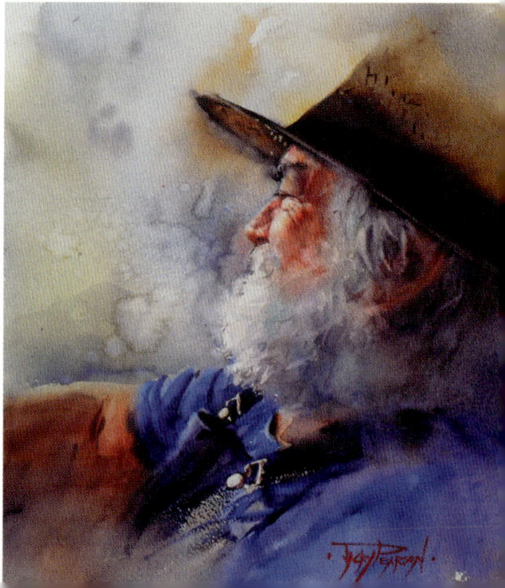

Principles and Elements of Design

Composition is all about design and the best possible arrangement of the elements in a painting. Why one painting "works" better than another may depend upon the strength of the design. Here are a few guidelines to help you work out the best composition for your painting.

Think of the principles as what you want to make and the elements as your tools to achieve this.

WHAT YOU WILL MAKE	YOUR TOOLS
Seven principles of design	Seven elements of design
Unity	Shape
Balance	Color
Emphasis	Tonal Value
Rhythm	Line
Contrast	Edges
Proportion	Texture
Repetition	Rest Area

Ideally all of these principles are worth using, particularly unity, but aim to build up your compositional skills by focusing on each one in turn, using all the elements. The principles of design will be affected by some or all the elements of design. Treat this as a feedback loop. If your painting isn't working, go back to these principles and ask if you have fulfilled them all?

Unity

Unity is the most important principle of composition. The parts of your painting need a way of coming together rather than appearing as disconnected sections. Techniques that provide unity include an underpainting, use of a "mother color" (adding small amounts of the same color to other colors in the painting), and use of similar edges.

In this painting, I have created unity using color, with an essentially cool, analogous palette, with blues and greens balanced by dull warms in the foreground. I have abstracted the shapes of the hills so they blend together to create a unified feel. I have also created a potential rest area in the bottom left and only developed the lighter tonal values.

Edges within the painting are soft and they lead the eye from one to the other. "Endeavour Inlet" 2025, Indian cotton and gesso.

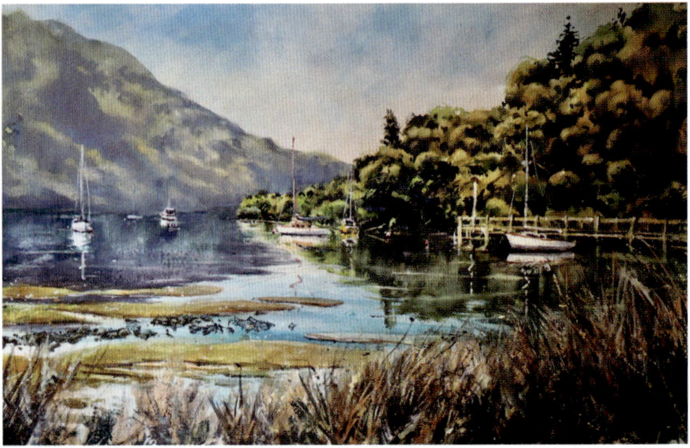

An underpainting really helps pull a painting together in terms of the light and the bright colors. Laying these foundations helps set up a good composition.

I started "*Endeavour Inlet*" as an underpainting to lay out the main light and bright colors. I allowed it to dry and then overlaid the darker forms on top. I did quite a bit of lifting and adding paint in the later stages. Compare this with the painting opposite.

A good way to unify a painting using a mother color was given to me by the late New Zealand artist, Tui McLauchlan (1915–2004). She told me to, "Put some sky color into the land and some land color into the sky."

In the underpainting for "Endeavour Inlet", I used a variegated wash to allow the colors to mingle together and form an abstract pattern.

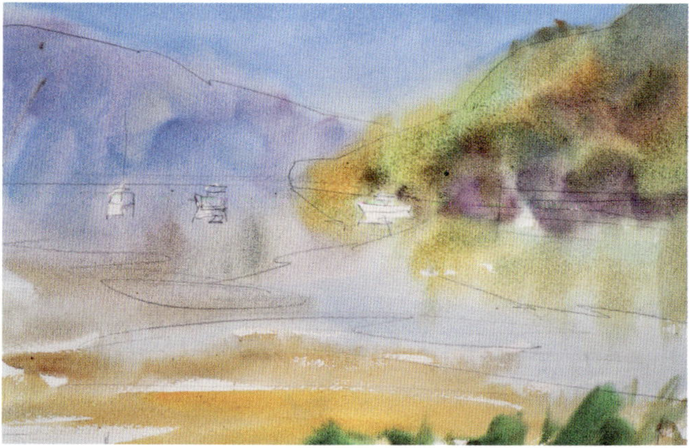

Balance

Balance is essentially about arranging shapes, and a strong composition will only have a few shapes. To identify these in your painting, squint at your scene through your eye lashes and you will see less color and more tonal values, which helps to see simplified shapes.

Choose your picture format first, as balance is affected by the format of your painting.

1. Landscape gives the most stable feeling and, unsurprisingly, suits a classic landscape scene. It is very flexible and the easiest format to work with.

2. Portrait is less stable and suits a subject like a portrait, which might move at any moment!

3. Square can be useful but hard to arrange elements within it.

4. Circular and oval formats have a contemporary edgy feel. It can suit some subjects.

Within your chosen format, create a series of thumbnail sketches to decide on the best composition.

DIVISION OF PICTURE PLANE

Generally, it is good practice to divide major areas of your painting unequally. I do this by approximating the Golden Ratio with a 60/40 split (or 3/8 and 5/8), which produces a more natural look than thirds. Start a painting by lightly drawing two horizontal and two vertical lines across your paper in this division. At least one horizontal and one vertical can be used.

Composition set up lines based on 40/60 Rule. You can add focal points at intersections.

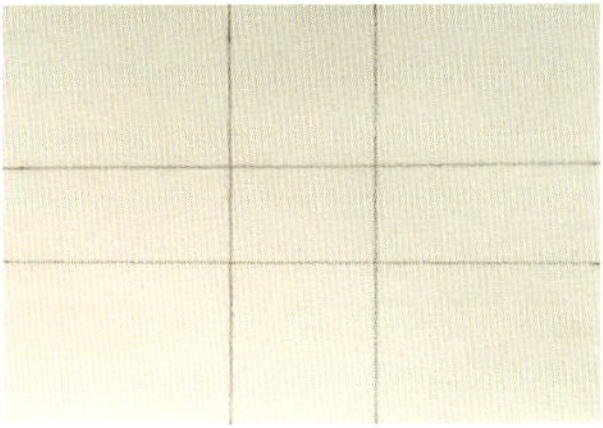

A typical division might be where the sky meets the sea (horizon line) or a line of a bank (as in the painting below). Place your focal points at the intersections. For balance, have one main focal point and then place a lesser focal point either at the diagonal intersection or the side intersection.

WHAT IS THE HORIZON LINE?

The horizon line (not to be confused with the skyline) is a horizontal line from your eye to your subject, perpendicular to your body. If you are sitting or standing on a cliff, the horizon will still be at your eye level.

REST AREA

Every painting needs a place for the eye to rest, and you can use balance and the division of your painting to achieve it. The rest area in the painting below is the blue-green water and is a relief to the eye from the busy brushstrokes of the river bank and trees.

"Quiet Fishing" 2019, cold pressed illustration board.

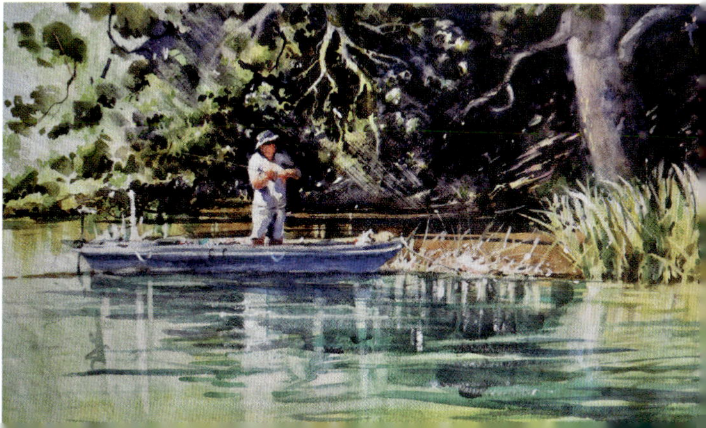

Emphasis

Use emphasis to draw the eye to the main subject of your painting, also known as the focal point or focal area. Use light against dark, cool against warm, dull against bright, and soft edge against hard edge to make that part of your painting stand out.

In this painting, I used a Golden Ratio spiral (like a nautilus shell) to help me decide where to emphasize the rolling wave. I wanted a way for the eye to travel around my painting but come to focus on the falling crest of the wave, where light meets dark, and hard edge meets soft edge. You can buy Golden Ratio calipers or templates to help you work out where to place elements.

"Splash!" 2022, Langton Prestige rough.

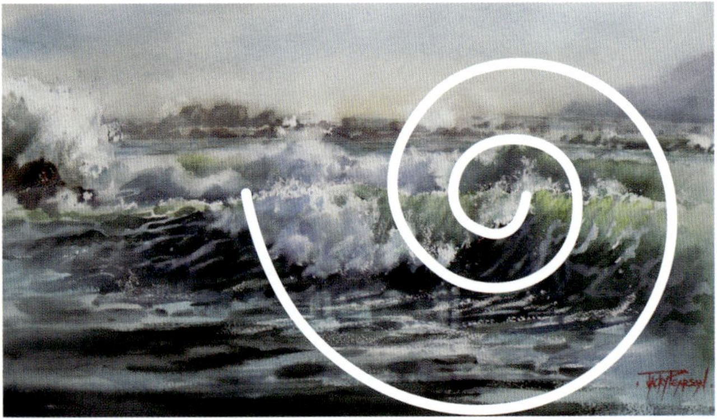

Rhythm

Rhythm is the movement within a painting, created by how elements are arranged and spaced.

USE OF LINES

Use imaginary lines to create movement and flow in your work that will take the viewer on a journey through your painting. A horizontal line, for example, gives a strong sense of stability, and draws the eye across the painting, great for a horizon line. A vertical line is less stable and can be used for trees and boat masts, drawing the eye up and down, as well as to your focal point. A dynamic or angled line gives a sense of movement and can also relieve the eye when there are strong verticals and horizontals. A curvy line can add to the flow of your painting, giving a gentle or casual feel, such as for a river or a path.

The variety of lines in this painting creates a busy feel.

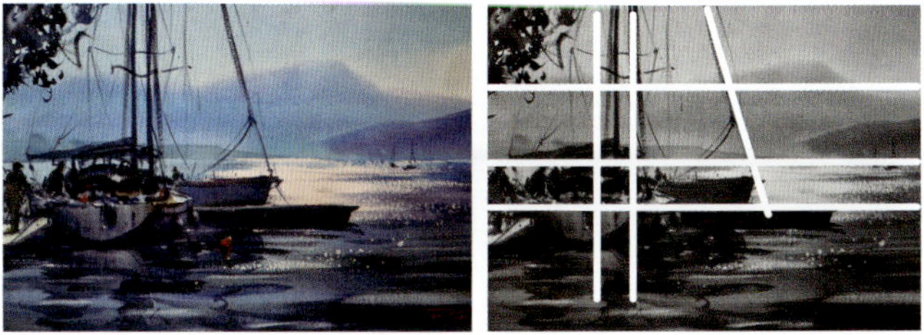

LINE DIRECTORS

Never underestimate the power of lines in your painting to direct the eye. Line directors, in "S," "Z," "L," or "X" shapes, allow the eye to travel to the back of the painting. Intersections of the lines can be placed in the Golden Ratio of the painting. The shapes of lines will also have a strong say in the emotional interplay between your painting and the viewer.

Spending time planning your painting pays dividends and is often underrated. Use thumbnails and trial paintings to establish lines, blur what you don't need, and focus on the main elements.

An "S"or "Z" shape is easy on the eye.

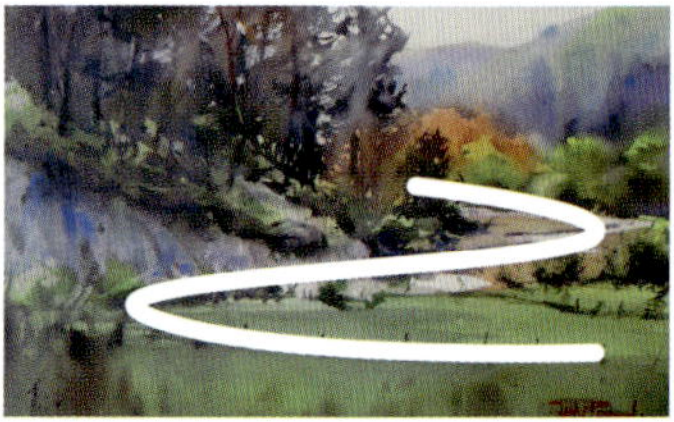

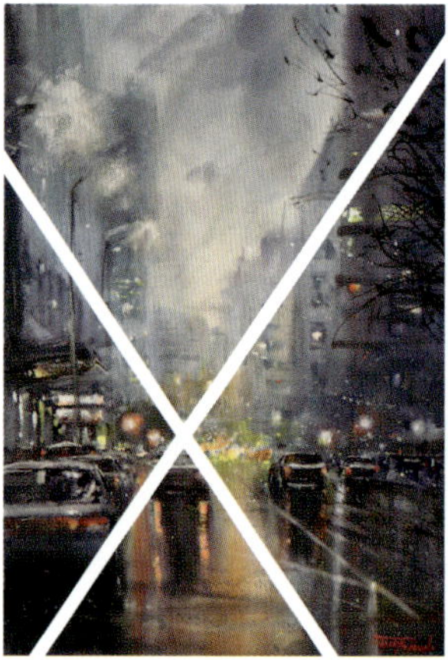

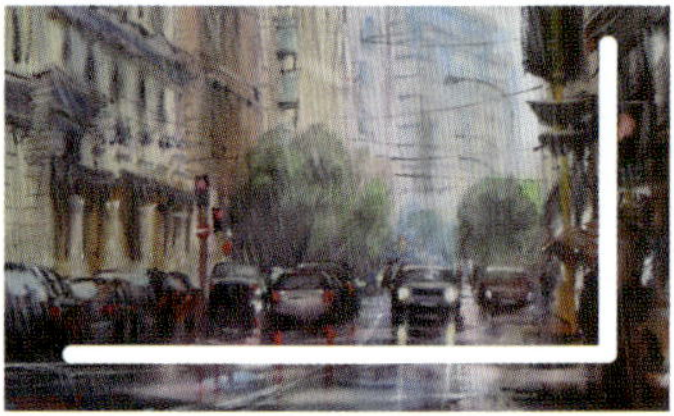

"X" shapes draw the eye to the back of the painting.

"L" shapes lend themselves to street scenes.

Contrast

This principle is the contrast between any element, which creates excitement. You be the judge of how much excitement your painting requires—you may want a calm look with more subtle contrasts.

Contrasts include: light and dark tonal value, cool and warm color temperature, bright and dull chroma, hard and soft edges, transparent and opaque pigment, small and large scale, horizontal/vertical and wavy lines, and textures.

COUNTER CHANGE

Value is the most powerful of all contrasts. Positive and negative shapes next to each other help create a pattern. This is known as counter change. Here, the figure in this painting stands out against a dark background. A subject might also have many counter changes along its periphery: dark against light, light against dark. Look, for instance, at places along the shoe mender's sleeves.

"The Shoe Mender" 2024, Langton Prestige rough.

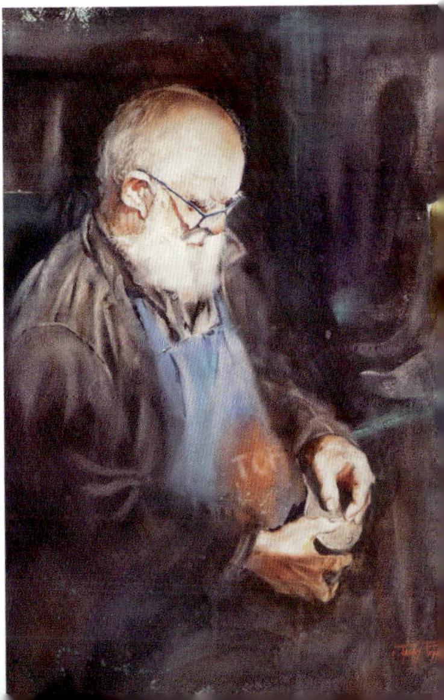

Proportion

Proportion is about putting objects in their proper place to make a believable scale. Use the following tactics to create depth and a way to travel into your painting.

ATMOSPHERIC PERSPECTIVE

The atmosphere distorts visible light and scatters blue wavelengths, as well as blurring and dulling colors. Base your distant subject(s) on a blue color to allow it to recede, and use the following elements from the background to the foreground:

1. Tonal value: light to dark.

2. Color temperature: cool to warm.

3. Chroma: dull to bright.

4. Edges: soft to hard.

Light, cool, dull colors and soft edges are used to create a sense of distance on a horizontal and vertical plane. As the painting comes forward from the distance, or from the top of an object, use darker, warmer colors and harder edges. A useful rule to remember when using colors is that blues recede and warms come forward. See Atmospheric Values in Chapter 6 for more on this.

STACKING

Stacking, where one object is placed behind or in front of another, creates the strongest form of depth and perspective. It is often overlooked but so important. In the painting, *Kangaroo Valley*, I added defined tree branches to the foreground, overlapping the whole scene. This allows the eye to see through to the back of the painting and emphasizes the distance.

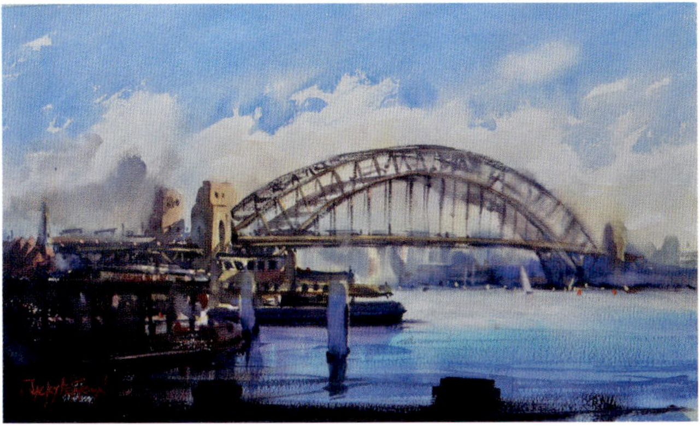

Here, I used different perspective tactics to create a sense of scale and distance, including atmospheric perspective to draw the eye to the back of the painting. "Sydney Harbour Bridge" 2023, Langton Prestige rough.

"Kangaroo Valley" 2018, Khadi Indian cotton.

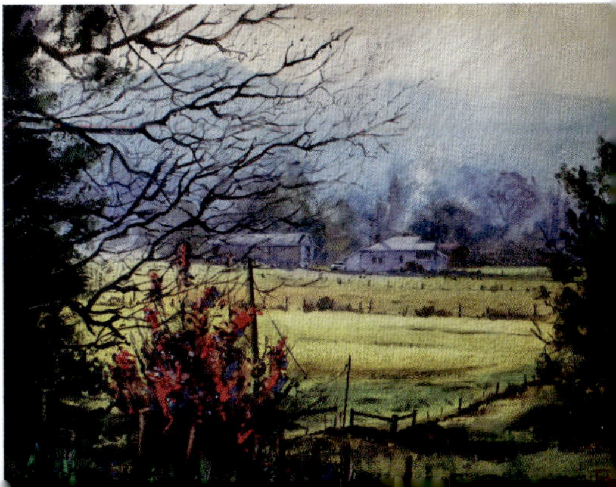

LINEAR PERSPECTIVE

Linear perspective is a big subject, but can be divided into single point, two-point, and multi-point perspective. On a horizontal surface, parallel lines will appear to meet at a vanishing point somewhere on the horizon line (a line extending horizontally across the view at your eye level). As artists, we can use vanishing points to create a realistic depth in a painting.

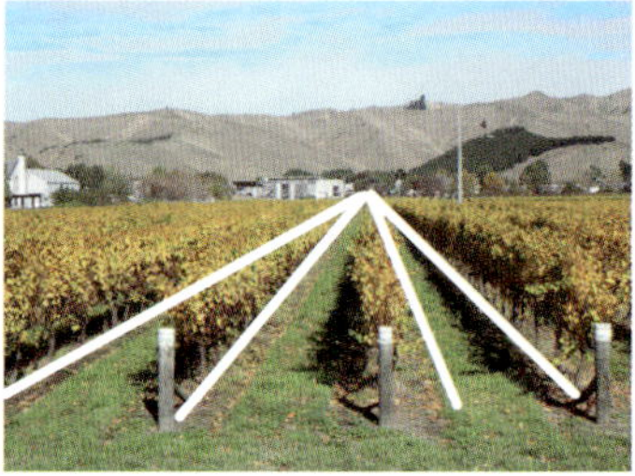

An example of single-point perspective.

One or both vanishing points may be off the edges of the paper. To find them, you can extend the lines by adding photocopy paper onto your watercolor paper. Place some string on a vanishing point and extend it across the paper to give you accurate perspective lines.

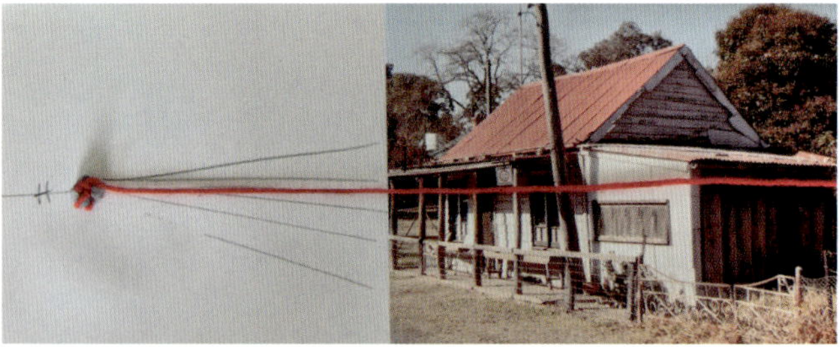

If you can see two sides of a building, you will see vanishing points 1 and 2 on your horizon line. Vanishing point 3, for the tilted roof, is above the horizon line.

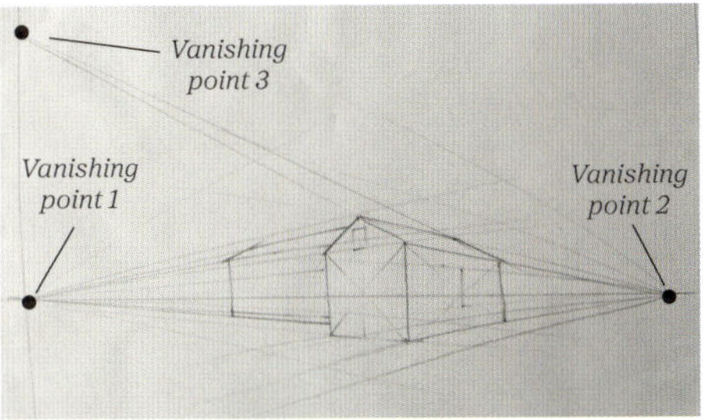

Repetition

Repeating shapes, colors, and values will reinforce your design and help create a unified composition. The repetitions don't have to be exactly the same, you can vary them to add interest. In this painting, I have varied the size, angle, colors, tonal values, and shapes of the headlands.

"Morning Light" 2025, Langton Prestige rough.

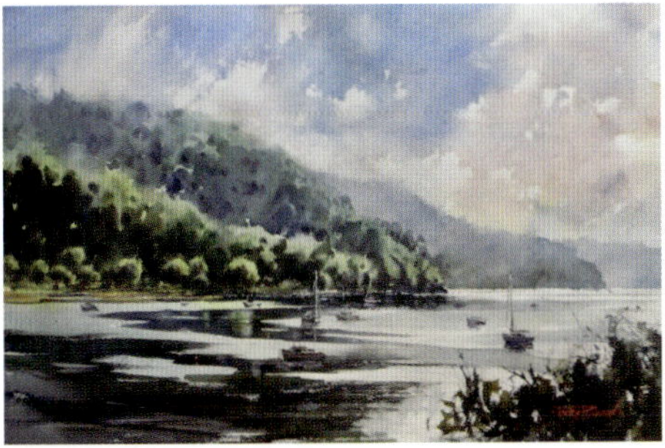

CHAPTER 6

Color Theory

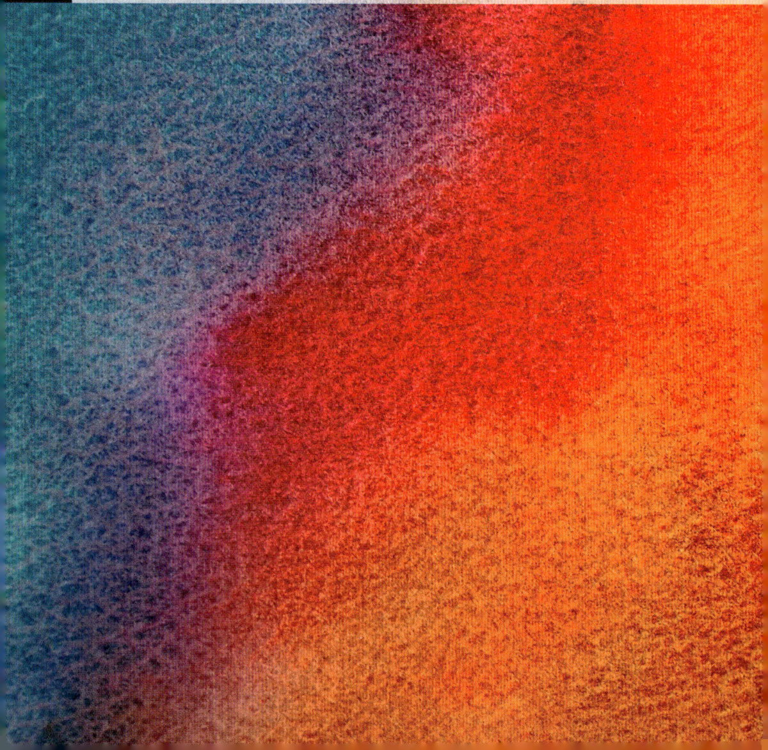

Exploring Color

Color provides the emotion in a painting but nature throws so many colors at us that it can be difficult to know where to begin. Understanding what color is and how it can be organized helps us make the best choices for our paintings.

How We See Color

White light from the sun hits a surface and that surface either absorbs or reflects certain wavelengths. It's these reflected wavelengths that the human eye can detect and translates into color.

Our eyes have two sets of cell receptors on the retina: rods and cones. Rods detect the lightness and darkness of a color. Cones detect long, medium, and short wavelengths, sending a signal to the brain, which

A leaf showing a cool side (at the top) and a warm side (at the bottom).

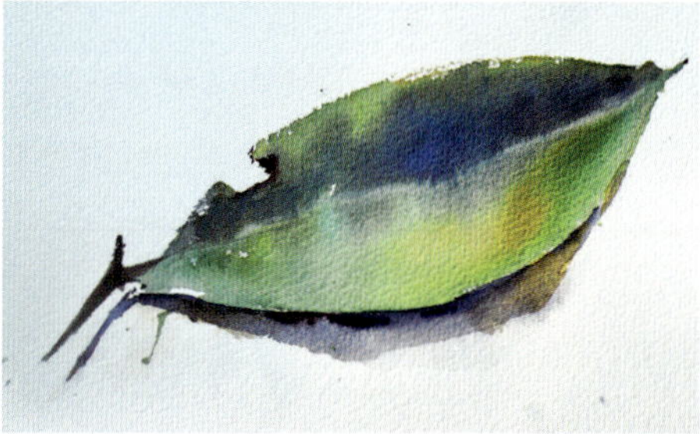

translates them into red, green, and blue respectively. Yellow is made by firing our green and red receptors. Everyone has a slight variation of this process, so it's important to develop a palette of colors that pleases you.

The leaf in the painting opposite is mainly green because more green wavelengths are being reflected to our eyes than other colors. There is some yellow in the painting because the chlorophyll (green) in that spot on the leaf is breaking down. Our eyes pick up this rise in yellow wavelengths and our brain translates it as a yellow color.

Munsell's Color System

At the turn of the 20th century, US artist and art teacher, Albert H. Munsell developed the best way to understand color. After seeking advice from top scientists, he defined color using hue, value, and chroma, and these are fundamental to painting.

1. Hue: the name of the color, such as red or yellow. Colors can be warm or cool, known as color temperature. Cool colors are blue, green, and violet, and warm colors are yellow, orange, and red. Cools recede and warms appear nearer.

2. Value: colors have their own value on a gray scale. In its most concentrated form, undiluted yellow is lighter in tonal value than red or Cobalt Blue.

3. Chroma: the dullness or brightness of a color. Synonymous words are intensity, saturation, brilliance, vividness, or purity. This is not to be confused with relative lightness of value.

Hue

Knowledge of the attributes of hue are essential to creating emotional impact in your painting. The color wheel has become the basis for color theory because it shows color relationships and is fundamental to color mixing.

Cool: think ice, sky, and water for the colors blue, green, and violet.

Warm: think fire for the colors red, orange, and yellow.

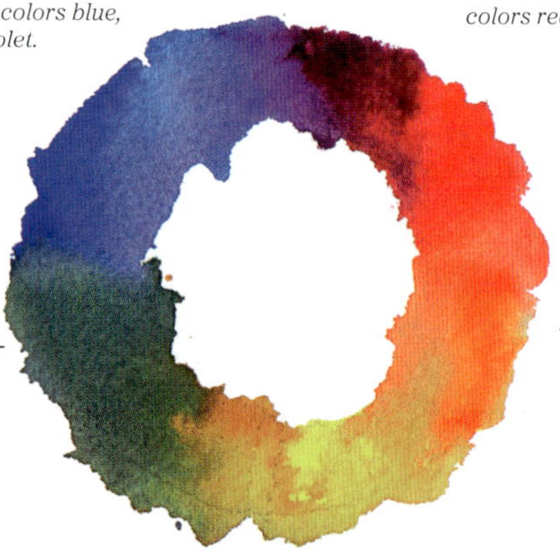

The color wheel is made up of:

Primary colors: red, yellow, and blue.

Secondary colors: a mix of two primary colors: green (red + blue), orange (red + yellow), and violet (red + blue).

Tertiary colors: a mix of a primary and a secondary color.

COLOR COMBINATIONS

Color combinations help in the development of a design.

1. Complementary colors are found opposite each other on the color wheel and enhance each other in terms of vibrancy, creating a dramatic effect. Examples include blue and orange, and green and red.

2. Analogous colors sit next to each other on the wheel and create a calm and gentle effect. Examples include green and yellow, and orange and red.

3. Triadic colors are three equally spaced colors, such as the violet, green, and orange.

1

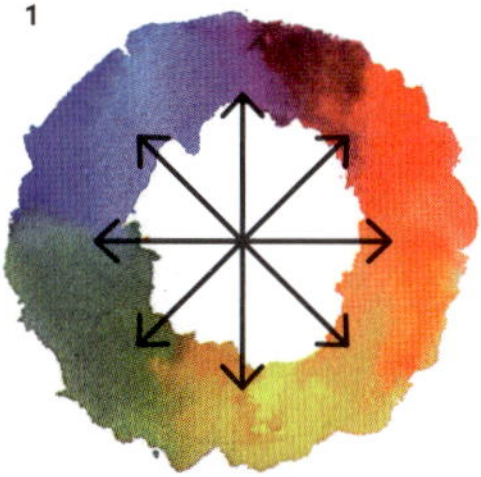

2

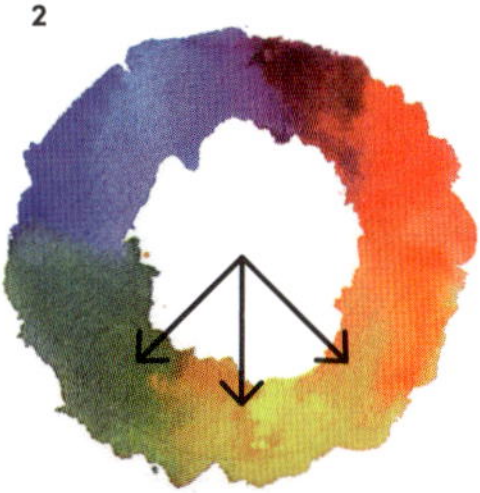

3

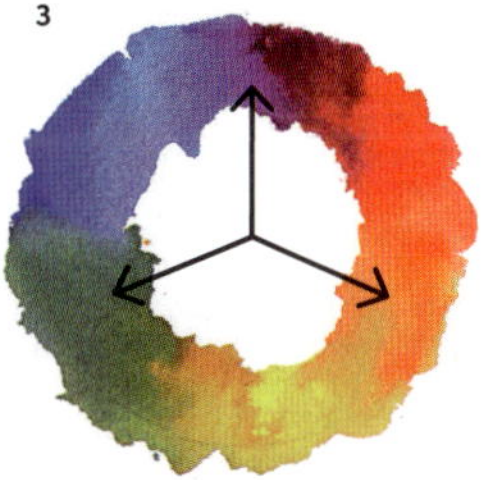

Value

Values (tonal values, or just tones) are the variations from light to dark of a hue, which allows us to perceive form, shadows, and space more strongly than hue and chroma. All colors can be assigned a value relative to each other, and they can all be made light to dark through dilution. Colors can be light, medium, and dark tones. About 70 percent of a painting might fall into the mid-tone range.

Seeing color as tonal values is essential. Squint at your work and reference during the painting process. This makes the details fade and you can see the values more clearly.

TRY THIS: MAKE A VALUE FINDER

On some watercolor paper, start with your thickest, darkest black and gradually dilute it with water so the last but one value is just dirty water and the last value is the white paper. I like to use nine values including the darkest dark and white paper, so there are enough but not too many values to develop. Now make a hole in each of the swatches with a hole punch.

Choose an area of color on a photo, or outside, place the finder's edge onto it and squint. Move the finder to the value that merges with the color. The hole helps to isolate the color value more precisely. Use the finder to compare what you are painting.

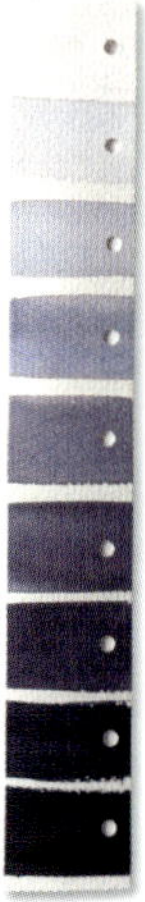

There are two ways of creating values. One is by diluting pigment with water for lighter values and using more pigment (less water) for darker values. A second is by utilizing the inherent value range of pigments, for example Ultramarine Blue, at the same ratio of water to pigment, has a darker value than Cobalt Blue.

ATMOSPHERIC VALUES

These make distant objects seem lighter than closer objects. In the photo below, lighter form shadows can be seen on the far mountains and get progressively darker as we move forward. Fingers of tree cast shadows can be seen across the fields in the foreground. Compare these darker cast shadows with more distant shadows.

A view from Crown Range between Wanaka and Queenstown on South Island, New Zealand.

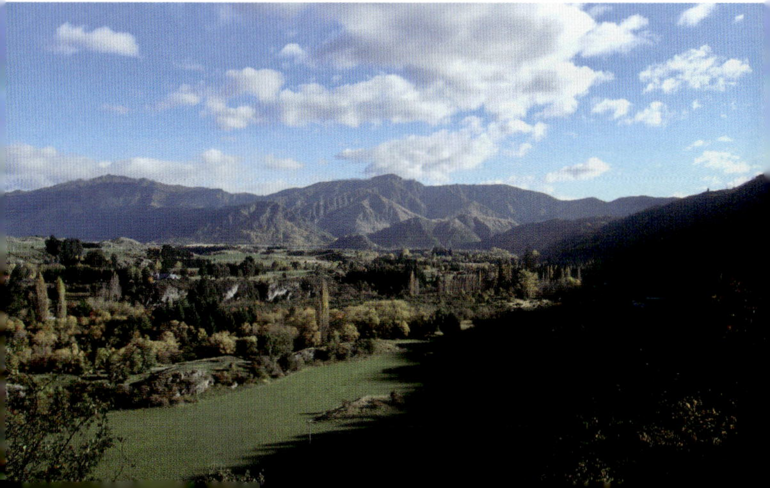

SHADOW VALUES

Shadows occur when an object blocks the passage of light. A form shadow is produced on the object when it is turned from the light. The object will also have a cast shadow that falls on an adjacent object. A low light source height will lengthen a cast shadow and, if high, will shorten it.

Form shadows on a rounded surface have soft edges. They will contain reflected light plus a darker cooler strip near to the light source edge known as the core (or crest) shadow. They contain:

1. Highlight: bleached out color of the direct light.

2. Lit area: the object has strong lighting on it but color is visible.

3. Halftone area: blurred transition next to the lit area, where the true color resides and appears more intense.

4. Core shadow: trapped light between the lit area and the reflected light. It is always a cooler and darker slither of shadow helping the eye create a sphere or rounded surface.

5. Reflected light: beyond the core shadow and taking up secondary light from another adjacent object.

6. Edge light: a slither of light on the edge of the object between reflected light and cast shadow.

7. Crevice shadow: where trapped light and no light reaches, so is very dark.

Cast shadows will have harder edges and not contain such strong reflected light as the form shadow, but it is often there. They contain:

1. Umbra and penumbra: darkest and semi darkest area, respectively, of a cast shadow.

2. Soft edges: on a cast shadow, its edges get blurrier away from the source.

3. Harder edges: nearer to the object, edges are firmer.

4. Terminator shadow: on the shadow edge, can be cool or warm.

5. Reflected light: contrary to some opinions, cast shadows do contain reflected light from the object casting the shadow.

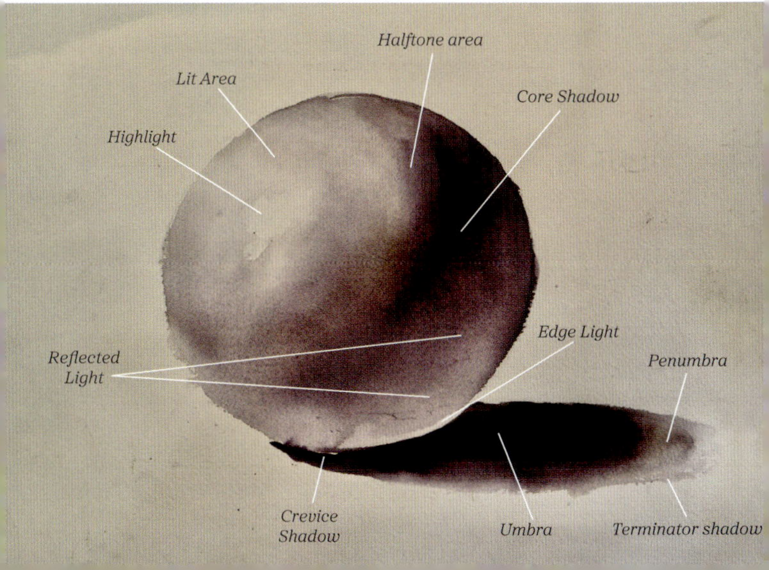

Color in Shadows

Color in shadows will depend on the angle of the surface or what surface they are falling on.

COLOR IN FORM SHADOWS

A form shadow contains not only value from reflected light from adjacent objects but color too. I took a photo of a duck and, while I was painting, I realized I'd captured an almost complete visible spectrum of colors in order down its form shadow! Under the duck's neck is the influence of the blue sky, then as the chest comes around, there is influence of the grass and finally the yellow, orange, and red influence of the legs.

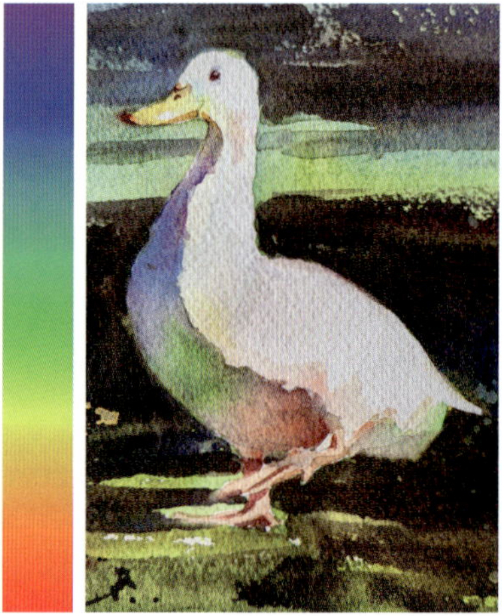

The form shadow of this duck shows the full visible spectrum from blue on the head to reflected red and orange legs.

COLOR IN CAST SHADOWS

A cast shadow will pick up the color it is falling on. Reflected light is less obvious than in a form shadow but is often found in the cast shadow.

1. Here the cast shadow of the tree looks dark orange. A cast shadow on grass will appear a darker version of the grass.

2. These mountain shadows are taking on a darker version of the cobalt blue sky.

3. Cast shadows from the hand contain colored reflected light.

Although the drama of light and dark effects captivates the eye, it is also the beauty of color and light in the depth of shadows that make a great painting.

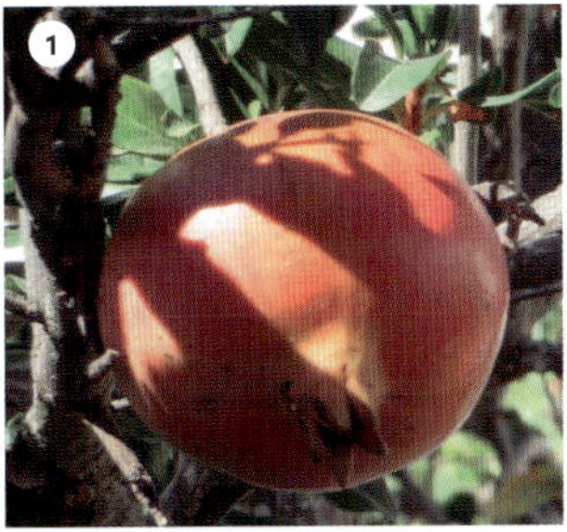

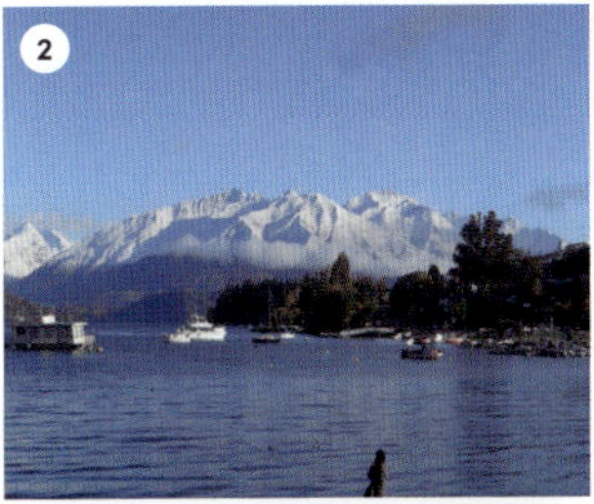

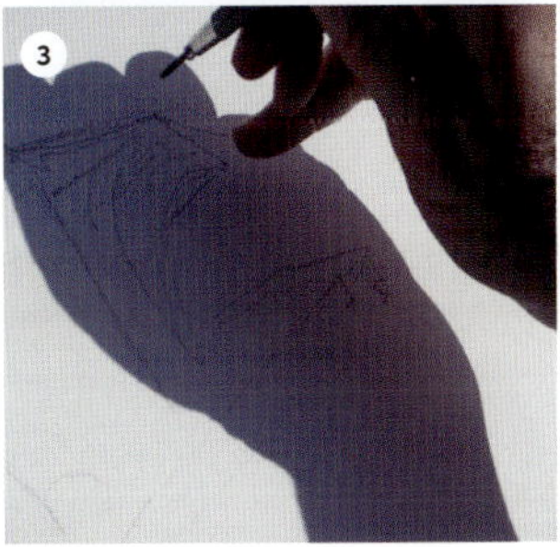

Chroma

Chroma is often ignored by artists or just confused with tonal value. Most of my paintings are about 60 percent dull colors and 40 percent bright colors. It depends upon the feeling I want to convey, of course, and I decide on the proportion in the planning stage of the composition. Dull colors allow me to pin point the focal area, for instance. I can surround an intense, single pigment with mixes that don't compete for attention. I am not after neutrals in these dull colors, just a low intensity.

When creating distance, it is important to avoid using high chroma pigments, such as Viridian Green. No matter how dilute, they will always try to reach forward and spoil the sense of distance.

Placing dull low chroma grays next to Lemon Yellow, a high chroma yellow, enhanced its chroma value. "Sounds Sunset" 2023, Langton Prestige rough.

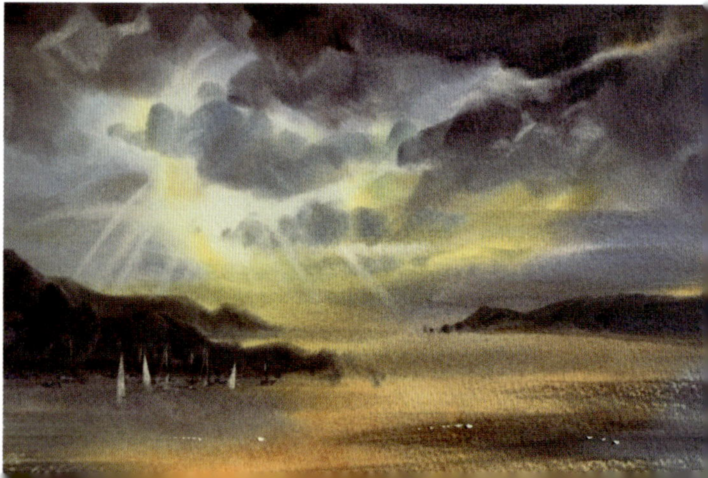

TRY THIS: SIMULTANEOUS CONTRAST

This is when a color appears to change depending on what other colors it is next to, and is one of your most important tools to use to emphasize an area of a painting, such as the focal point. Place one or more of the contrasts of hue, value, and chroma next to each other to create a powerful optical illusion. I often use all three. Experiment and see how these elements are all influenced by what they are adjacent to.

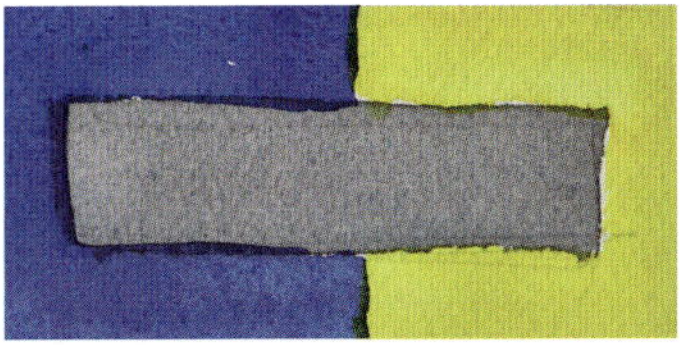

Here the warm blue and bright yellow surrounds a neutral value. The surrounding colors change our perception of hue, value, and chroma!

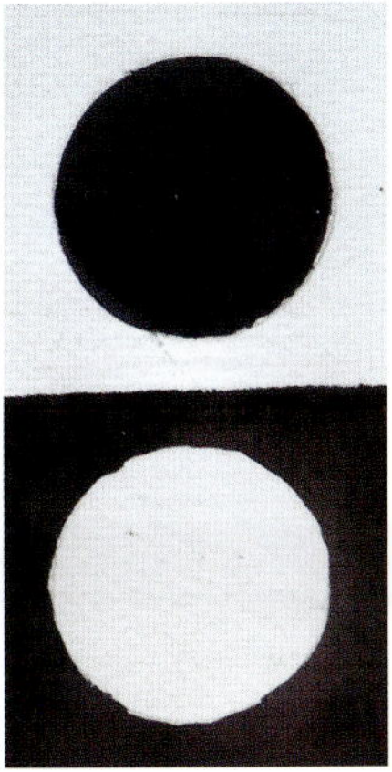

These circles are the same size. Placing one value against another completely changes our optics. White expands against a dark background and dark recedes against a white background.

CHAPTER 7

Color Mixing

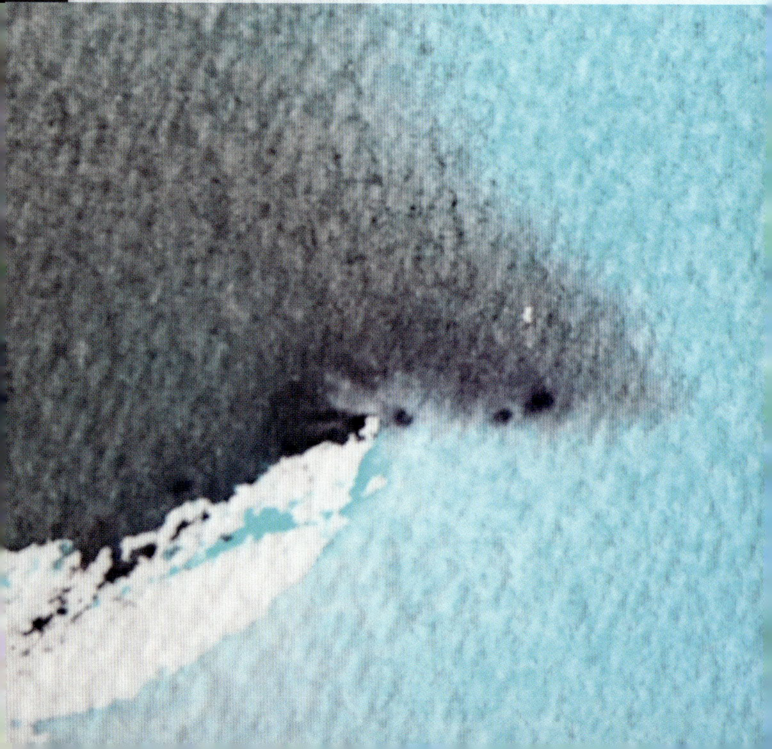

Creating Colors

Producing luminous and glowing colors is what is so appealing about watercolors. Learn the personality and individual characteristics of your paints for the effects you want. I hope this chapter gives you a color mixing strategy that sets you free to explore and develop your own unique palette.

Mixing in Practice

Use the three key elements of hue, value, and chroma, which we looked at in the previous chapter, when mixing colors. Train your eye to see colors as cool or warm temperatures, relative values, and the relative brightness and dullness. Remember, all colors are influenced by their proximity to each other. The more you train your eye, the easier it becomes.

Let's find the best colors to use for these rose petals. Mix as much paint as possible on the paper, wet-on-wet. This will give a lovely glow and fluid look to your washes.

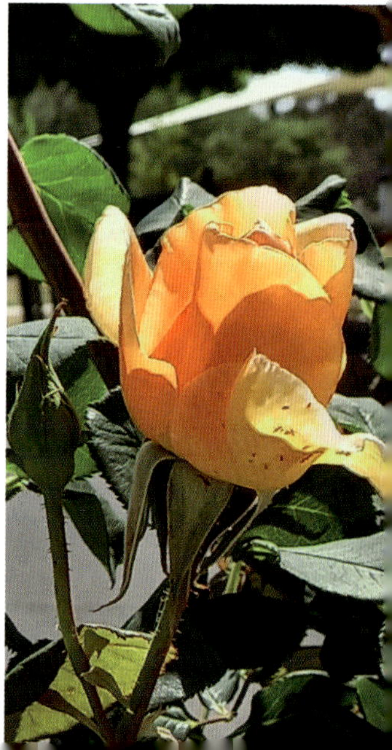

1. Hue: I matched sunlit areas to cool Lemon Yellow (left) and warmer Indian Yellow (right).

2. Value: I diluted the colors on the paper to allow for variations in tonal value. Thicker paint is a darker value and watered down paint is a lighter value.

3. Chroma: I added Cadmium Red, a high chroma color that stands out in any situation. This red is apparent in some transitional areas between light and shadow.

4. Shadow: the shadow colors on these rose petals are best represented by the analogous (yellows and oranges) and complementary (violet) sides of the color wheel. Wet-on-wet, I added Cadmium Red, Magenta, and Raw Sienna, let those mingle a little and then added some Cobalt Blue into the Magenta for the violet I could see in places.

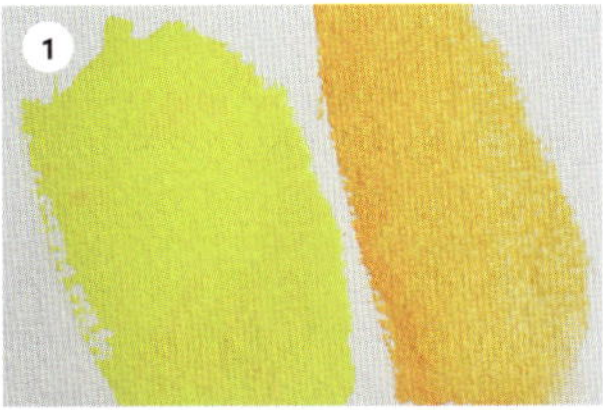

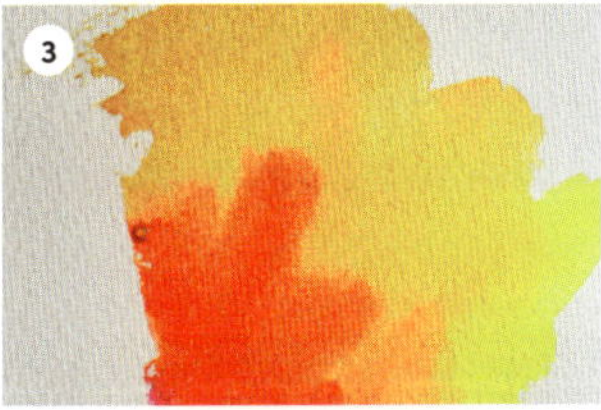

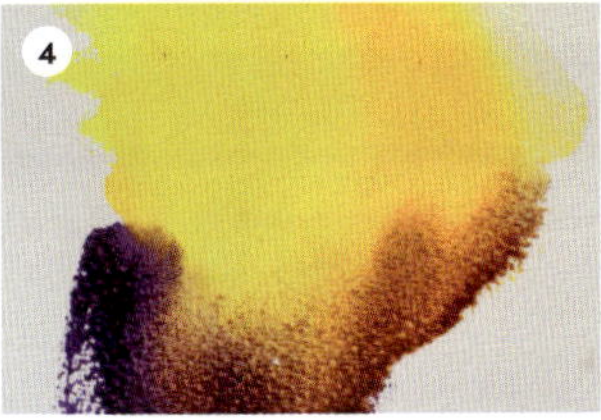

Choosing Your Colors

All color families (blue or red, for instance) can be categorized as having a cool or a warm color temperature. However, they may be a little biased (or lean) towards the other. For example, Ultramarine Blue, though in the cool family, is a little on the red side compared to other blues like Cobalt Blue or Cerulean Blue.

Understanding the cool and warm bias for each hue will enable you to mix a bigger range of wonderful colors with a relatively limited palette and create better space, form, and energy. Also, if you mix cool and warm biased primary colors together, you will usually get cleaner and brighter secondary and tertiary color mixes. After this, you can add a third primary color, cool or warm, to create gorgeous grays.

Use the tables below to identify the properties of some popular hues to get you started.

WARM FAMILY	HUE	VALUE	CHROMA
Cadmium Red (PR108, O, G, S)	WW	M	HC
Quinacridone Magenta (PR122, T, NG, S)	CW	D	HC
Cadmium Orange (PO20/PY35, O, G, S)	CW	D	HC
Pyrrol Orange (PO73, T, NG, S)	CW	L	HC
Raw Umber (PY42, O, G, S)	CW	M	LC
Burnt Umber (PBr7, T, G, NS)	WW	D	MC
Burnt Sienna (PR101, T, NG, NS)	WW	M	MC
Raw Sienna (PY43, T, NG, NS)	WW	L	LC
Lemon Yellow (PY175, T, NG, NS)	CW	L	HC
Indian Yellow (PY83, T, NG, NS)	WW	M	MC

KEY

Highly transparent (T) or opaque (O).

Granulating (G) or non-granulating (NG).

Staining (S) or non-staining (NS).

Hue: Warm (W) or cool (C). Preceded by W or C to show the hue's bias.

Value: Light tonal value (L), medium (M), or dark (D) in concentrated form.

Chroma: Low/dull (LC), medium (MC), or high/bright (HC).

Paint codes are given after the hue name (see Pigments in Chapter 1).

LIMITED PALETTE

This color palette will get you started. A huge array of colors can be achieved by mixing these hues.

Cool Hue Family: Cobalt Blue *(cool cool)* and Ultramarine Blue *(warm cool)* a warmer blue, and Viridian Green *(cool cool).*

Warm Hue Family: Magenta *(cool warm)* and Cadmium Red *(warm warm)* a warmer red, Lemon Yellow *(cool warm),* Raw Sienna *(warm warm)* a warmer yellow, and Burnt Sienna *(warm warm).*

COOL FAMILY	HUE	VALUE	CHROMA
Ultramarine Blue (PB29, T, G, NS)	WC	D	MC
Cobalt Blue (PB28, T, NG, S)	CC	M	HC
Cerulean Blue (PB35, O, G, NS)	CC	L	LC
Phthalo Blue (PB15, T, NG, S)	CC	D	HC
Cobalt Turquoise (PB36, O, G, S)	WC	M	LC
Cobalt Turquoise Pale (PG50, O, G, NS)	CC	L	HC
Indanthrene Blue (PB60, T, NG, S)	WC	D	MC
Viridian Green (PG7, T, NG, S)	CC	M	HC
Green Gold (PY129, T, NG, NS)	WC	M	HC
Ultramarine Violet (PV15, T, G, S)	WC	D	MC

Paint Threads

Here is a useful way of getting to know your palette's capabilities.

Create a paint thread that starts with Ultramarine Blue and ends with Lemon Yellow.

Have your board on a 15-degree angle, allowing the paint to flow and gently merge with the next color. Do as many versions as you wish, adding colors randomly or systematically. Make notes at the side of color combinations you love. Make a little "card set" on watercolor paper with color threads and pencil in color names.

Experiment, for example, by mixing a very high chroma color, such as Pyrrol Orange or Pale Turquoise, with a duller, low to medium chroma color such as Raw Umber or Ultramarine.

Colors are influenced by so many factors including adjacent colors. See how the same color looks in a different thread order.

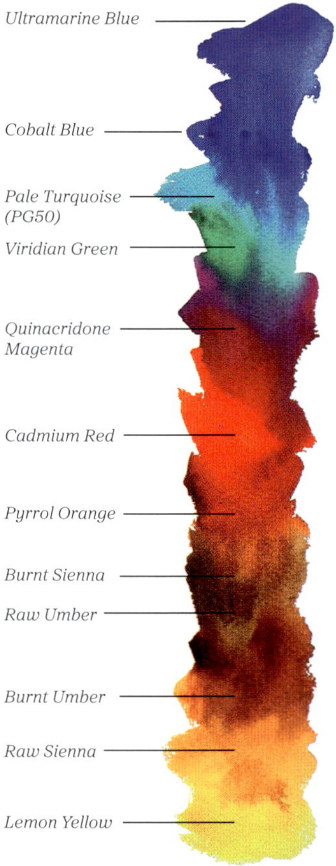

Pigment Characteristics

Watercolor paints are so versatile with so many useful nuances. When made wet, different effects can be achieved depending on the pigment grain size, shape, and weight. Certain hues can be relatively more transparent, opaque, staining, and granulating (sedimentary), as shown in the Color Family tables.

TRANSPARENT PIGMENTS

All watercolors are transparent, but some pigments are more so. They tend to be the most useful for wet-on-dry glazing because they won't crowd out the previous dry wash. Transparent colors have more finely ground particles and tend to throw an even covering on the paper, which will create lovely, even washes. The particles are finely ground enough so light can penetrate and reflect the white of the paper beneath the paint. When layering several thin washes, drying in between layers, transparent pigments are the most useful to create a glow.

Transparent pigments, mid painting. "Hari Hari" Langton Prestige rough.

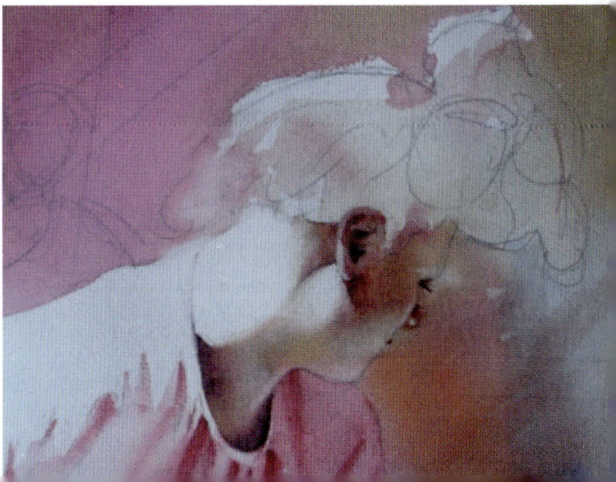

OPAQUE PIGMENTS

Some watercolor paints are relatively opaque. The particles are bigger and will return the light from the granules rather than from the white paper beneath. They are very useful for areas that need an illusion of texture, like rough ground, or creating a statement. In wet-on-wet glazing, opaque paint can create beautiful textures. However, be careful when painting wet-on-dry glazes, as too much can overwhelm the layers beneath.

GRANULATING PIGMENTS

Pigment sinks or floats. If you are using rough or cold pressed paper, heavier paint will settle in the hollows (or tooth) of the paper and the lighter paint will float. Transparent and opaque paint can be granulating, also known as sedimentary. When paint granules do sink into the tooth, you will notice it leaves a beautiful sediment. Experiment with brands and types of paper for this effect. I love it! Rough paper, well wetted, will create the best effects. As a rule, cool paints sink and warm paints float. In the example, the Quinacridone Magenta is coming to the surface and the Ultramarine Blue sinking.

Non-granulating pigments react smoothly and evenly with water. They tend to cover the paper equally, with little or no variation in color and texture.

STAINING

When dry, a staining color will be harder to lift, but while it's still damp, it can be fairly easy to do this. They are very useful for adding as an under color where you want to lift out shapes and have a color remain beneath rather than white paper. In this example, I have previously painted Viridian Green and dried it, added a layer of dark over it, and scraped this off to reveal the green stain underneath.

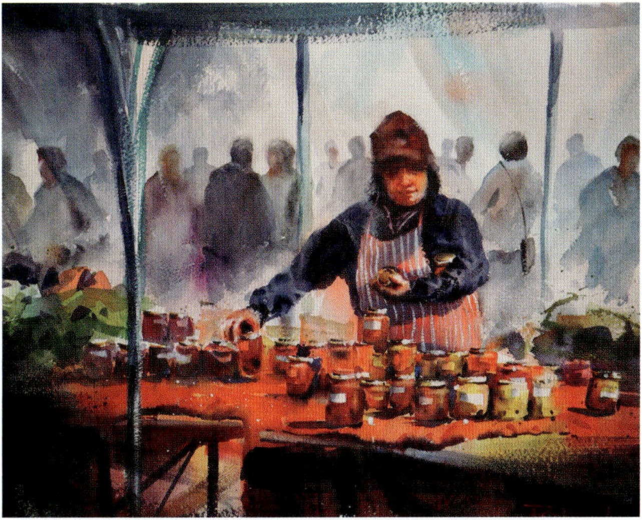

Opaque pigments can make a statement, like the Cadmium Red in this scene.

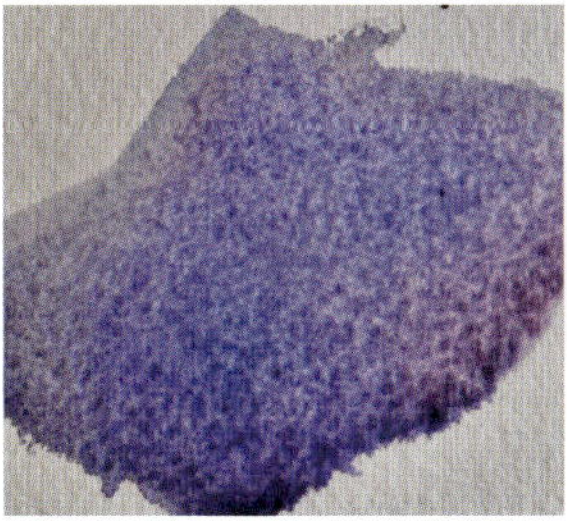

Granulating pigments

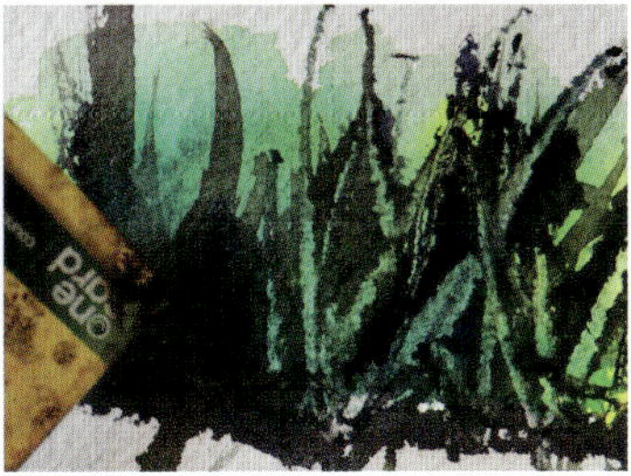

Staining

Mixing Greens

Green is arguably the hardest color to mix, so here's a useful way to achieve a range of greens.

Start with the intense, high chroma (bright) Viridian Green, as it is easier to dull a color than make it more intense. Now add different yellows to get to the green that you want. The yellows will determine the color temperature, value, and chroma of the final green. To dull the chroma, add Magenta, which is the complementary color of green.

Viridian, on its own, doesn't depict nature well due to its high chroma, so use it only as a mix. However, it can be used in small amounts to liven up a painting.

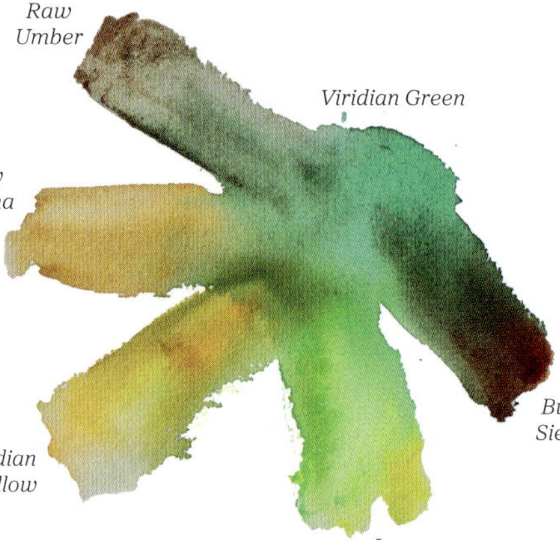

Homemade Black

Darks are an important part of a painting. I find ready-made blacks homogeneous and unnatural. Darks for shadows need to be transparent and clean looking. I use the following color combination as a base black on my palette. I can warm it by adding extra Burnt Sienna, cool it by adding Cobalt Blue, lighten the value with Raw Sienna, or raise the chroma and brighten it by adding Pale Turquoise (PG50).

HOW TO MIX BLACK

Create a mix of mainly Ultramarine Blue and a small amount of Burnt Sienna and Quinacridone Magenta (or any cool red). Squeeze the paint in the well of your palette and stir it with the end of your brush. It will be a very dark purple rather than a black. Note colors will vary from brand to brand.

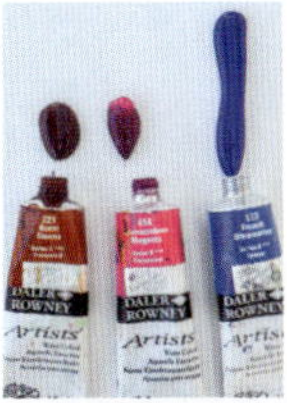

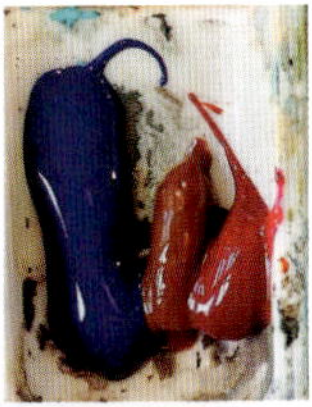

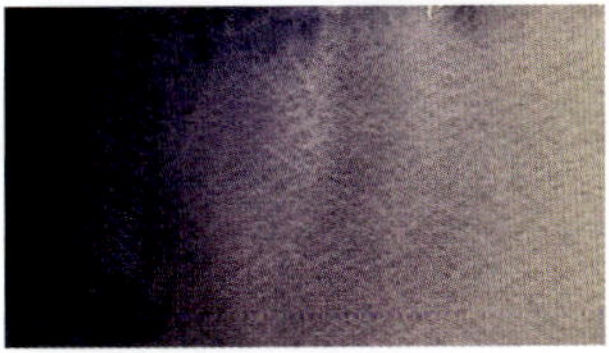

Other options include mixing Pyrrol Orange and Ultramarine Blue (50 percent of each), or Magenta and Viridian (50 percent of each).

To make a glowing dark, to add variety to your shadows, partially wet the paper within the shadow area. Add a few brush marks of Burnt Sienna and then, wet-on-wet, smother homemade black on top.

Vibrant Grays

Technically, if you mix two colors together you are graying a color. Three colors will further neutralize the hue. Gray can make up to 70 percent of a painting and enhance a good design. As it is a blend of colors, gray can be a perfect counter to make a single color stand out. A gray is never neutral and can lean towards the warm or cool side of the color wheel, depending on what it is next to and how it is mixed.

The colors making these gray clouds were applied separately on the paper, very wet (No. 1 and 1.5 mix), so they are optically mixed. This creates more life than colors mixed together on the palette. "Harbor Sailing" 2019, Langton Prestige rough.

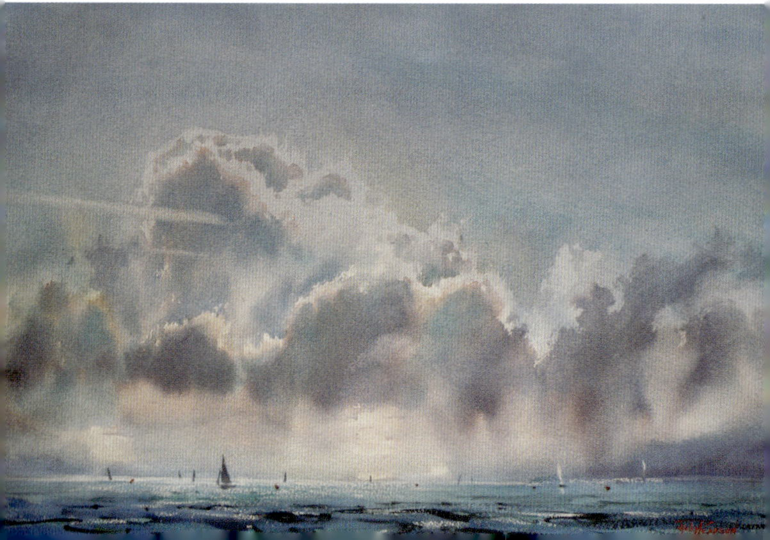

HOW TO MIX GRAYS

Complimentary colors, opposites on the color wheel, make beautiful grays when mixed together: blue and orange; yellow and violet; red and green.

Mix the colors unequally on your palette and/or mix them unequally on the paper. If your gray is looking too neutral, it is probably because it is over mixed and the colors are of equal strength. Here are a couple of examples of mixes that I use to make gray. When these colors merge, you will see a variety of different grays.

1. Cobalt Blue and Quinacridone Magenta, overlaid with Raw Sienna.

2. Cobalt Blue and Pyrrol Orange PO73, overlaid by Raw Sienna.

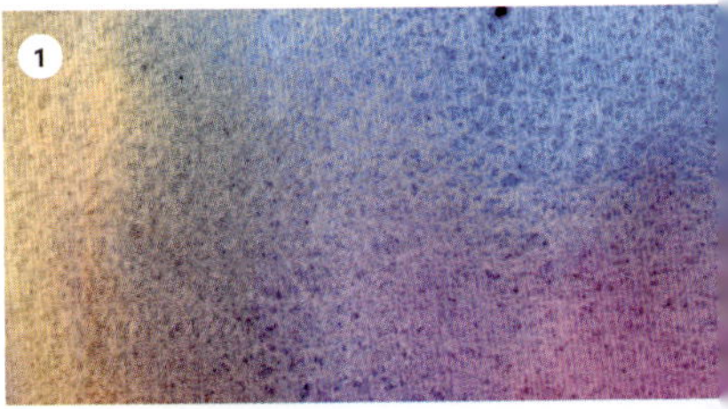

CHAPTER 8

The Painting Process

Making Your Marks

Planning is the key. Do not start a watercolor painting from scratch and expect it to turn out as you thought it would. A writer makes drafts and polishes their work into better prose; a watercolorist must use this same process of revision. Major alterations are hard to achieve halfway through the painting. To mitigate this, I always do a draft painting no matter what! This gives me a more in-depth understanding of brushstrokes, color, and composition. And know that you can never completely master this watery medium—there are just too many variables! This chapter takes you through my own painting process, one stage at a time.

"Letting the Paint Dry" 2025, Arches rough.

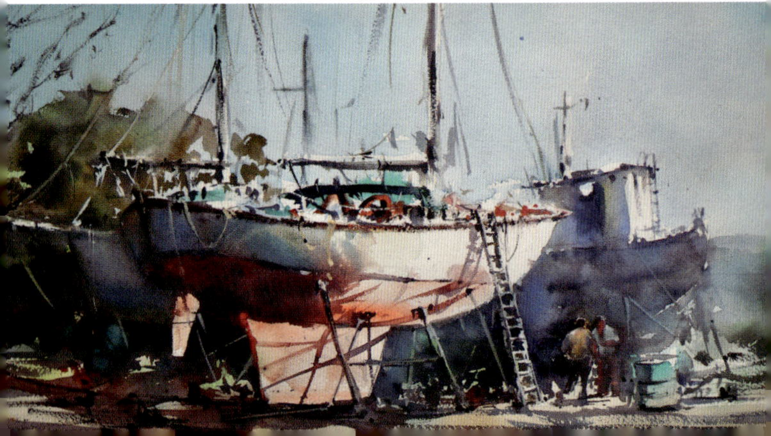

Quick Draft

Start by creating a two-minute thumbnail for the placement of objects. Then, give yourself a maximum of 30 minutes to make a draft painting. Use this to figure out composition, values, and unity, and the general feeling or emotion that you want to convey. Get your tonal values sorted and the rhythm of the brushstrokes.

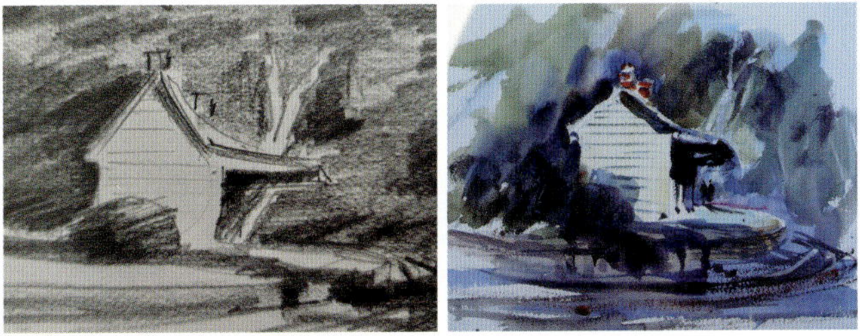

Quick drawing or tonal painting sketches make you look harder at the subject's characteristics and understand your scene. If you spend too long on these, you lose spontaneity and it might even put you off doing these important "thinking-out-loud" sketches.

Three-Stage Painting Technique

Once you are happy with your draft, it's time to create the final painting. Start by drawing up: draw lightly on the paper with a soft pencil, such as a 2B or 4B, so it doesn't damage the paper and can be erased easily. Your drawing should be accurate but loose, which allows for spontaneity of brush marks when painting. There are then three main painting stages to create the final work.

1. The underpainting: this stage knits the painting together, providing both unity and a mood or sense of feeling. It will largely provide the watercolor glow. Work out what the "mother" color is, in other words the underlying color that creates the mood. It might be warm or cool. Patchwork the colors wet-on-wet. Start with the light and bright colors first. Paint all the intense and lightest values in your subject and, apart from missing out where you want white paper to remain untouched, slosh the paint on (No. 1 to 1.5 mix, occasionally No. 2 mix). Let it mix and mingle all over the sheet of paper, one color into another. Use a large flat brush or pointed mop brush.

2. The middle: this is where the bulk of values and shapes, form and cast shadows are created and clarified. As a watercolor painter, you need to become expert at painting around ("cutting in") objects and areas that stand out from the background. Leaving white paper, next to dark paint, will contribute to a lively painting and can be used to direct the eye. You can also add positive shapes (darker toned areas), such as large shadows, that will ride over the top of the underpainting but be transparent enough to allow the original color to glow through.

3. The detail: this stage can often be the jewelry that makes the painting interesting. Now you can add details, such as figures, little bits of white scratched out, or highlights painted with white gouache. Be aware that you can over-bling your painting! Less is more, so be judicious about the amount of detail and where in the painting it is required. A rule of thumb is to keep the detail in the focal area and hardly any in the background.

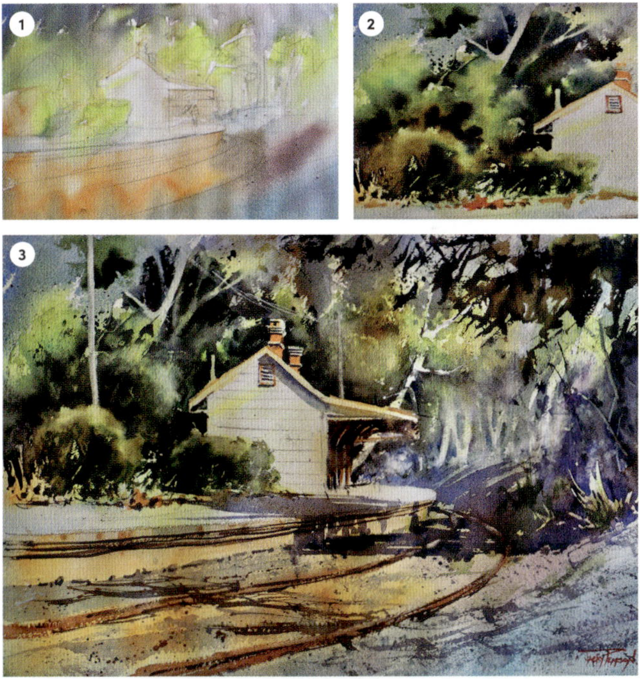

"Old Railway Station" in Kandos, Australia, Langton Prestige rough.

Seascape Walk-Through

Let me take you through how I painted this image of Nobby's Beach, in Australia. A scene like this requires a sense of movement, like you've captured a moment, and needs to have plenty of wet-on-wet brushwork.

QUICK DRAFT

Draft paintings are a must for me in my painting practice. I make a few drafts to understand the painting before starting the final version. In this case, it helped to get into the flow of lines for the waves. The colors I used here were Ultramarine Blue, Viridian Green, Raw Sienna, Lemon Yellow, and cool Magenta.

TRY THIS: PAINTING WAVES

Think of a wave as a tube with spiral movement. To get into the flow of lines, practice these marks with your brush, following the black arrows.

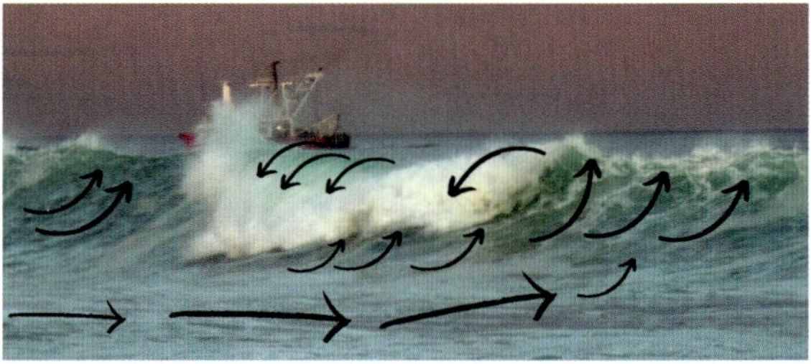

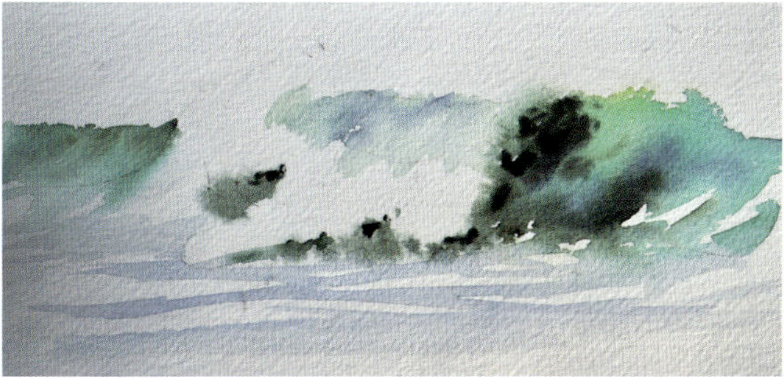

The quick draft gave me the time to work out the pattern of the complex waves, paying attention on how to create form and movement.

TRY THIS: TONAL FEATURES

Here are the tonal features to look out for when you paint any image. Horizontal surfaces will reflect the sky and be lighter. Vertical surfaces will be darker.

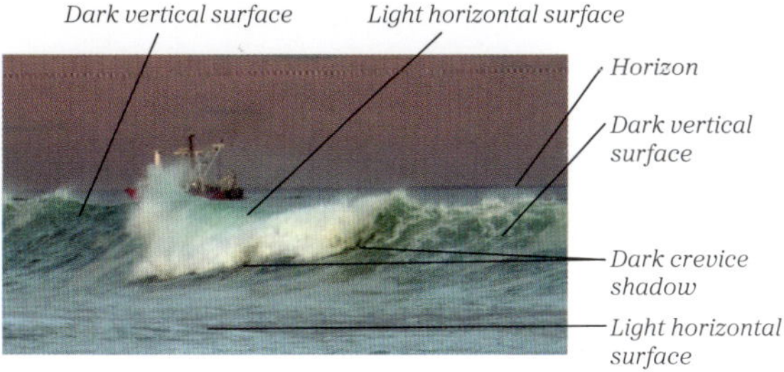

DRAWING UP

I loosely draw the wave but add the pattern for the strips of foam rising up the wave to the right. I then wet the paper back and front by putting the whole sheet under a running tap (yes, really). I lay it on my art board and it sticks to the board without slipping.

THE UNDERPAINTING

Sky: I start with the sky. While the paper is very wet, I lay on several thin wet-on-wet glazes (No. 1 mix) of Raw Sienna, Magenta, and Ultramarine, until the strength is achieved. Remember that watercolor dries lighter than when it is very wet, so make an allowance for this. I end the glazing with Magenta as the final wash, as it is the last pigment laid down that makes the difference. While the sky is wet, I sprinkle some table salt into it to add another dimension to the spray and foam. The pattern of the salt develops over time as it absorbs the water.

Waves: I apply paint between the white rivulets on the rising part of the wave using Viridian Green, and blue colors with yellow on the thinner top of the wave. I leave plenty of white strips, as I will glaze them later with a blue-gray using a medium-sized pointy wash brush. Whilst it is still wet, I use a flat brush to push some of the green back and soften some of the edges. Viridian is a staining color but very liftable while wet or damp (see Lifting in Chapter 4).

I hold the painting upside down and, using a spray bottle, blur the top of the wave into the sky. Gravity naturally merges the colors into the sky.

Use a soft pencil for the drawing up and create a flow with directional lines. All these lines will come off when the painting is dry.

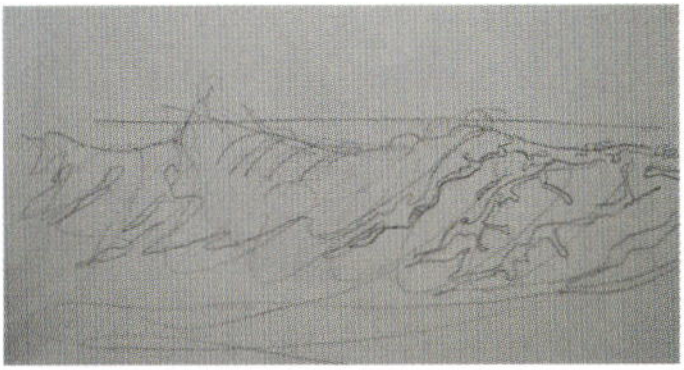

I dry some white spray areas and the rising part of the wave that needs some white patterns by dabbing with an old clean towel. Do not worry about the paper cockling. If you want to flatten it more, rewet the back of the paper.

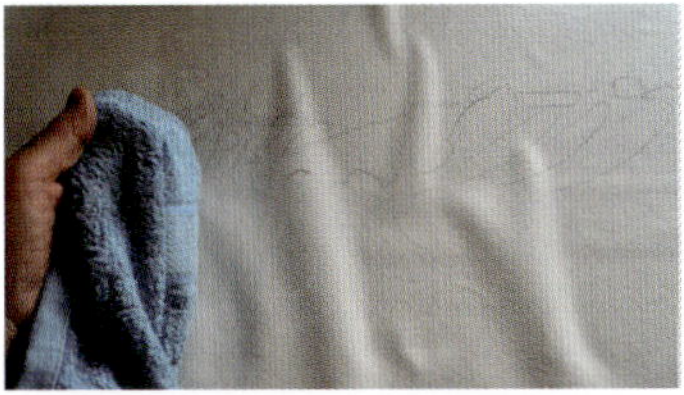

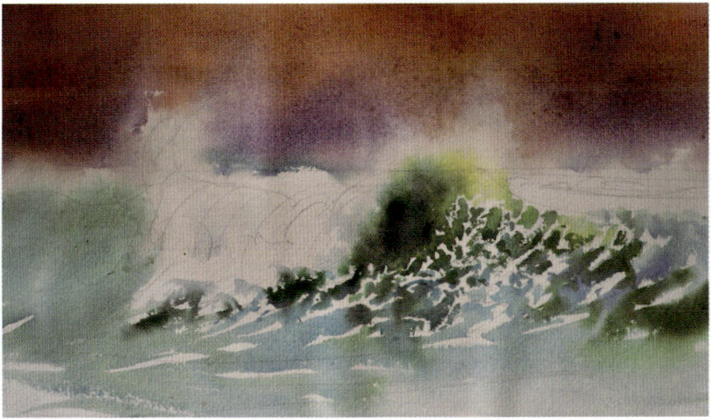

I used Quinacridone Magenta in the sky for a sunset color but dulled it with some Ultramarine Blue, so that the sunset didn't overpower the wave. The red is complementary to green, making the wave stand out.

THE MIDDLE

To create the large shadow under the wave crest, the wave must be dry. I then use a large pointed mop or a Hake brush to make as few brushstrokes as possible. I add violet (Ultramarine Blue and Magenta, mixed on the blue side) and create the shadow as the wave rises. This will gray the "white" rivulets.

Next, I make a mix, a thick Viridian and homemade black, and add it, wet-on-wet, under the white of the wave in a few places to give it depth and form. With my brush on its side, I scumble into the darker areas next to the wave spray to create a soft edge.

THE DETAILS

I soften and blend some edges, and using white gouache, flick in some white spray. The salt added previously will keep working till dry, then I can brush it off. I create the color and very pale value for the top of the wave tube. I create a feeling of movement by following the contours of the top of the wave tube and lightly scumbling a very pale blue-green (Cobalt Blue and Viridian, No. 1 mix). This part of the wave is not only facing upwards towards the sky, making it tonally lighter, but it is also full of spray, so making the color paler.

The foreground is also reflecting the sky and lighter in tonal value. However, I paint in some darker oval areas where the foam has spread, revealing the deeper water below. To finish off, I use more scumbling on the foam and develop the blanket foam in front of the wave.
In Chapter 9, you can see more ideas for finishing a painting, such as using sanding and adding white pastel.

The sky can stay wet, but the wave area needs to be dry to create shadows during the middle stage.

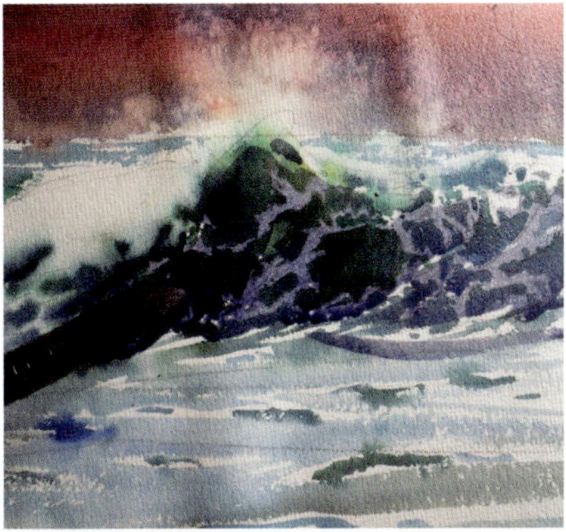

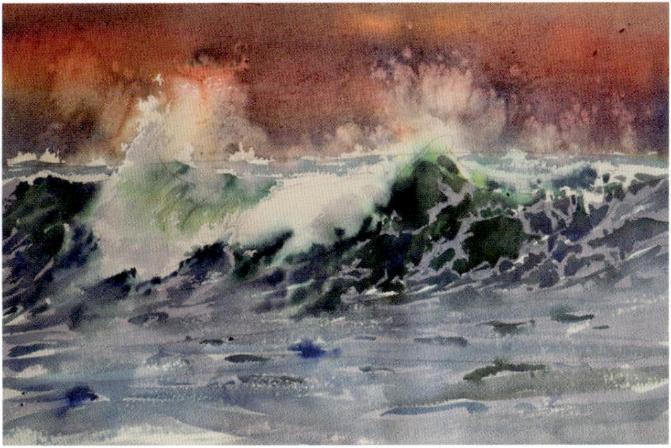

"Wave Demo" 2024, Langton Prestige rough.

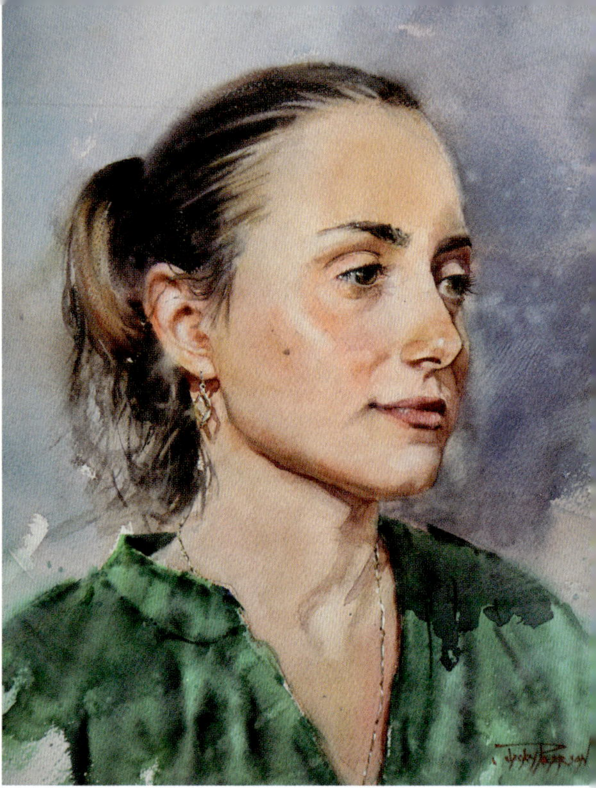

Portrait of Maryana Walk-Through

This is my lovely daughter-in-law, Maryana, and I have tried to capture her quiet strength and calmness. I have used soft edges to create a sense of "just about to move" to the painting.

TONAL QUICK DRAFT

I usually create my drafts in color, but in black and white, subtle shapes and paint thicknesses for tonal variations can be explored more closely. A portrait needs to have a fusion of soft and hard edges. Too many hard edges and you will have a face with no life, too many soft edges and the face will look insubstantial. It's also important to gain an understanding of how form and cast shadows work (see Chapter 6). It is always worth doing a 5-minute value sketch before the draft version to plan the composition.

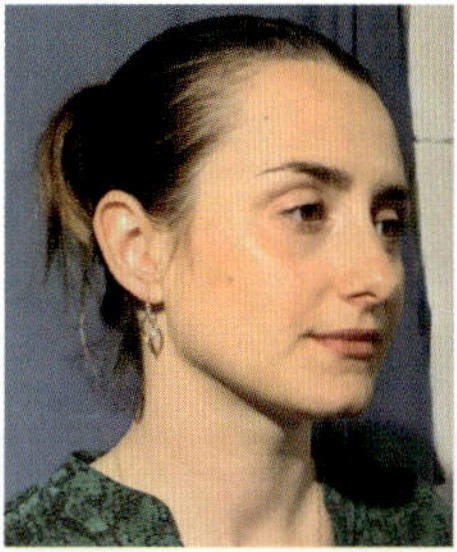

The draft painting helps me see the areas that are going to be light against dark and dark against light. I also decide where the hard and soft edges are going to be.

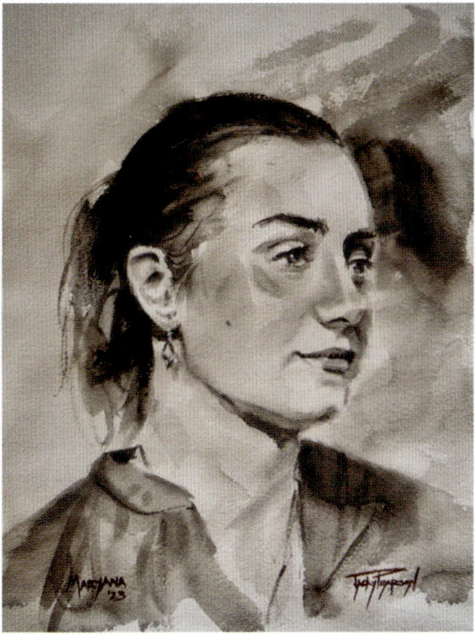

DRAWING UP

I start with a circle, adding a line for the eye axis that is about one third from the bottom of the circle. Add the chin line (a lower horizontal line), which is the same distance from the eye axis to the bottom of the circle. This will make the eyes halfway between the chin and the top of the head. You can do this for any head angle. I move onto the jaw shape next, which gives the beginnings of a likeness.

THE UNDERPAINTING

Starting with Ultramarine Blue, I develop a variegated No. 1 and 1.5 wash. I aim to finish the underpainting with more blue in the background and hair, and more of the warms, such as Raw Sienna, on the face, as well as some Cobalt Blue. I paint over the right eyeball in a Cobalt Blue and let it merge with the other colors. I tip the painting around to naturally merge the colors. It is a mistake to push paint around too much with a brush.

I like to get the background in quite early and integrate the head and the background. I do this in landscapes too. Blue added into the dark hair now serves as a bluish highlight later on. This is where I add plenty of brightness (chroma) into the underpainting. Remember that colors become less intense as they dry. Therefore, I can seemingly exaggerate the colors at this stage. I charge my brush with color and water for each color.

While the underpainting is still wet, I add a runny (No. 1.5) mix of Burnt Sienna and more Ultramarine Blue into the background. I flick splashes of water with my fingers to add texture the background.

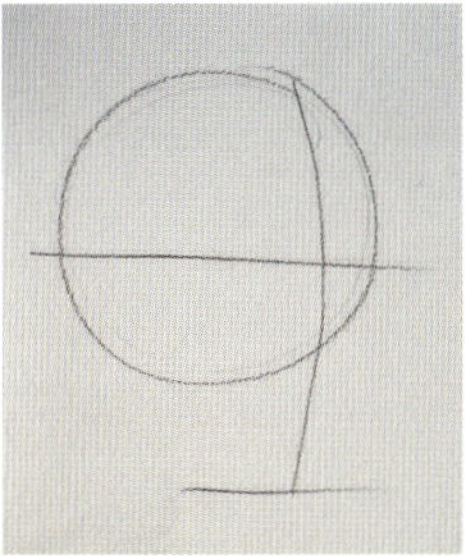

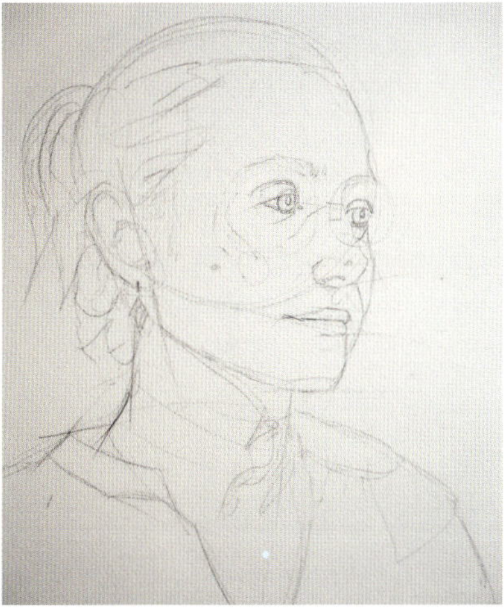

This universal template keeps the features in the correct place. Before painting, ease heavy pencil lines out with a kneaded eraser.

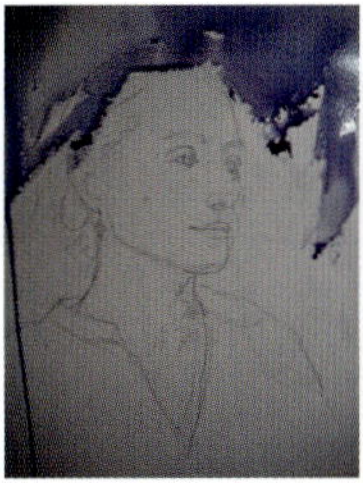

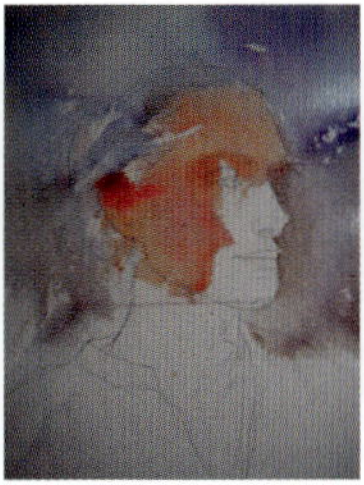

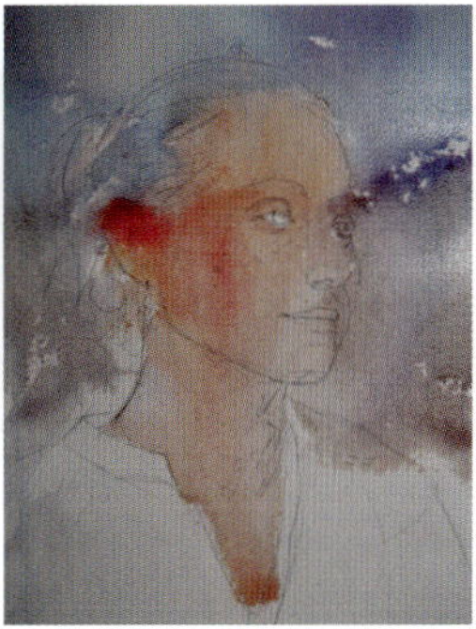

This sequence was painted with a leading wet edge with a bead as I add the next color. Each color is added side-by-side (variegated wash) with occasional colors dropped wet-on-wet on top of the wash beneath.

While the painting is still damp, I use thicker dark Burnt Sienna and Ultramarine (No. 2 to 2.5 mixes) for hair texture. I lift some hair highlights with a flat synthetic brush and allow the hair to blend in places with the background. At the same wetness stage, I increase the warm colors on the face, ears, nose, chin, and cheeks with No. 1.5 to 1.75 mixes of Raw Sienna, Cadmium Red, and Magenta. I paint around facial high points, such as the temple area, and lift the wet paint with a flat synthetic brush.

I then leave the painting to dry after this stage.

THE MIDDLE

Now I add layers of paint for the hair and features. The hair develops through lifting paint and glazing many times. Notice how the top lip is darker (shaded) and cooler (Magenta), where as the bottom lip is the reverse: lighter and warmer (Cadmium Red).

I use a flat brush (either a Hake or synthetic, size 1in/2.5cm), and lay on wet-on-dry glazes of Raw Sienna and Pyrrol Orange, in thin washes, to develop the contours of the face. Cadmium Red can be used in the nose tip, cheeks, and chin to make them appear to pop forward.

THE DETAIL

Details can make or break a portrait. With a flat synthetic brush, I develop the hair by softening and lightening high points where the light catches it. I give the ear a soft edge so that it appears to go back in space.

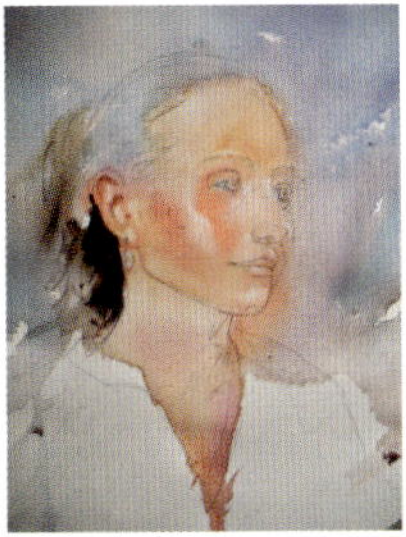

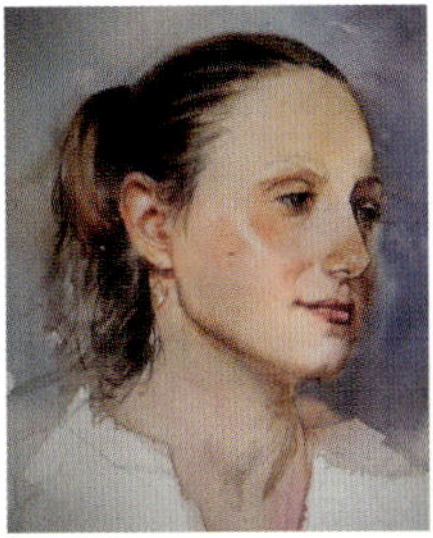

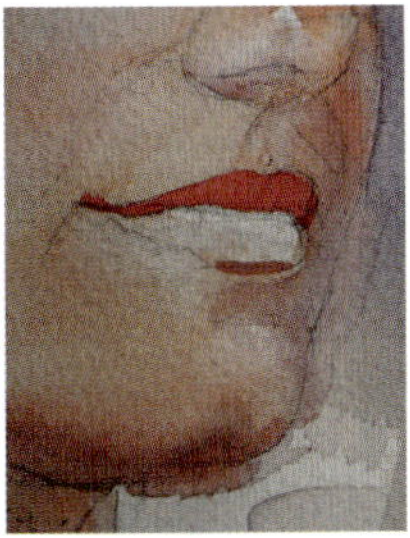

Use thick wet-on-wet paint (No. 3 mix) for the hair.

The painting is dried, then wet-on-dry layers and details added.

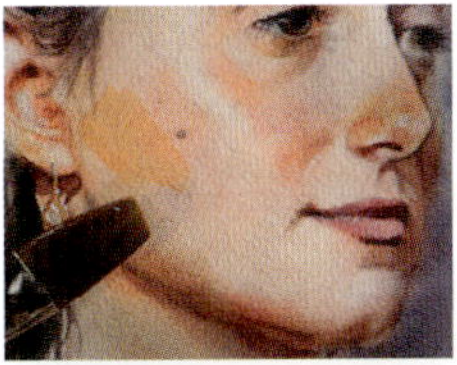

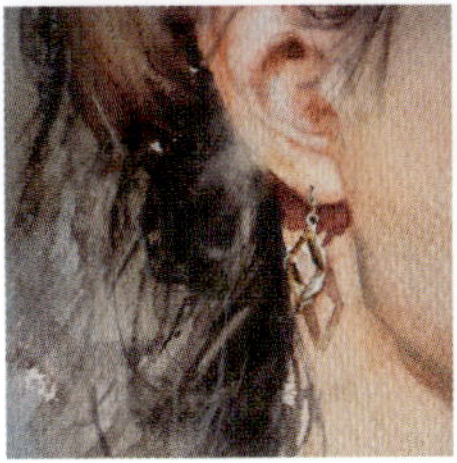

Add a warm shadow (never cool on skin) to make the earring appear to have form.

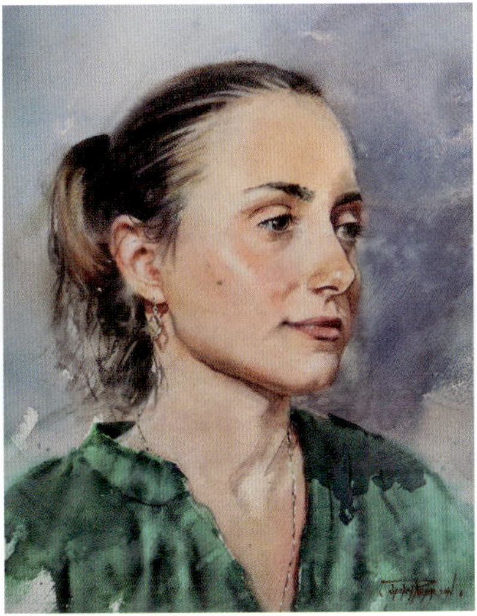

Adding Figures

Figures are so useful to add energy and scale in a painting. They can be added later or planned from the start. They can be detailed, or left as a loose impression. A figure is generally seven to eight heads per the length of the body. Make heads smaller rather than too big, and make sure the legs are half of the whole length.

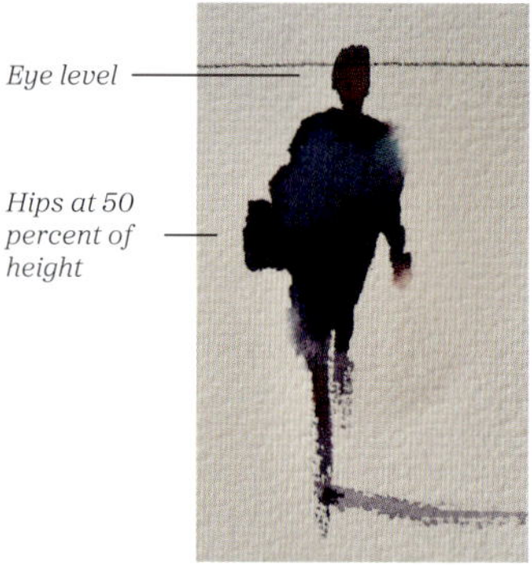

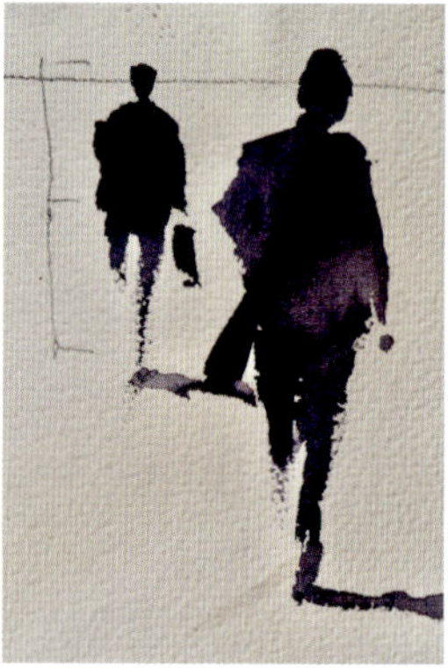

To add extra figures, assuming a horizontal surface, add a head of a different size on the same horizon line.

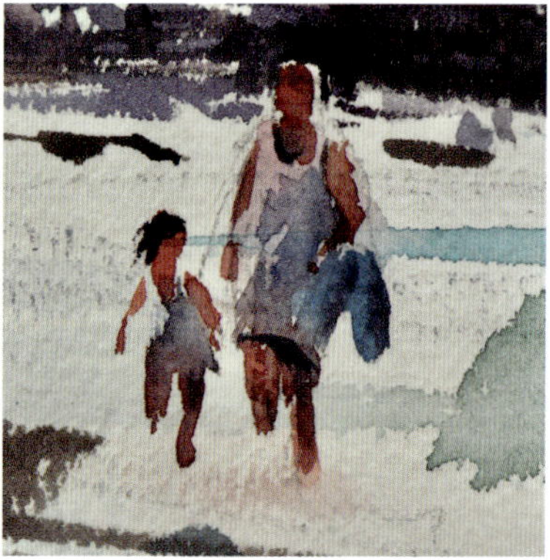

Children are below an adult's eye level. Other adults will be on the same eye level as you, give or take.

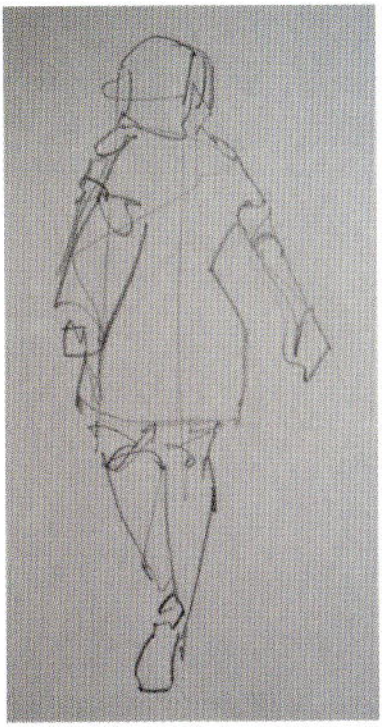

GIVE YOUR FIGURES MOVEMENT

Draw your figures gesturally. Keep your pencil on the paper while drawing and you will find some lovely unexpected gestures happening. Don't worry about the pencil lines as you can rub them out later. To create movement in a group or crowd, don't paint every leg and foot.

TRY THIS: PAINTING A GROUP

Paint a group of heads side by side, using No. 2 mix. Gradually add torsos, and create a bead by using enough water in the mix and slightly tilting your paper as you paint. The bead will keep the clothing together in distant and middle distant figures. It will also blend some of the figures together with one wash bleeding into the next wash from figure to figure. Drag the bead down the picture to form the legs.

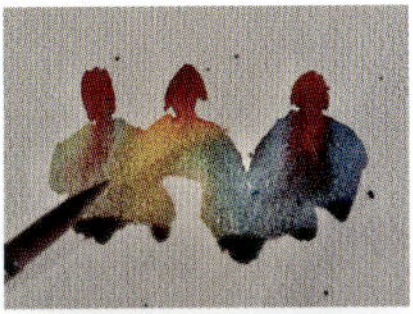

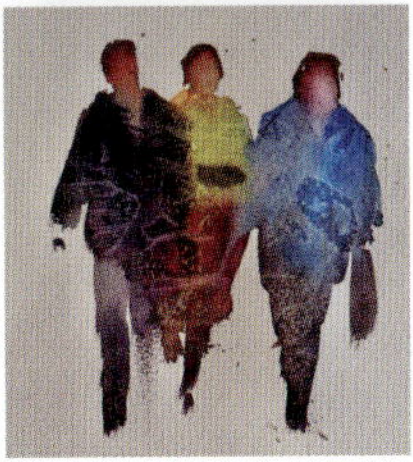

WALKING FIGURES

When a figure is walking towards you, or away, make one leg shorter and thinner. The far leg will also be darker due to it being shaded. To add light figures in a dark background, paint all the light colors and pale shadows first. Then, using a wet-on-wet approach, wet around the figures and add some thick dark paint (No. 2.5 or 3 mix).

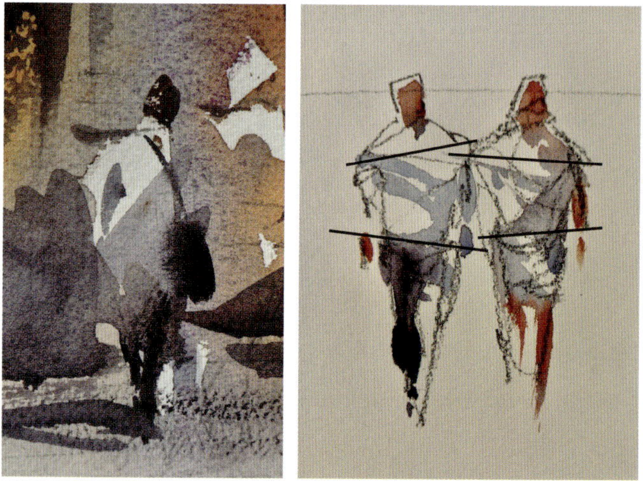

For walking figures, the angle of the shoulders opposes the angle of the hips.

WALKING SIDE ON

1. Paint within your gestural drawing. Use a spray bottle, or flick a few water droplets with your fingers, around the figure to make some variegated edges.

2. For details, add the thicker darks last. Remember you can always rewet your paper if you want a soft edge. It is important to rewet when the paint has been dried so you don't get a messy mark or a runback.

3. The shadow goes in last but paint it as soon as you paint the foot on the ground so it seamlessly continues, cool and dark near the foot, and paler and warmer with a softer edge further away. Make sure the shadow does not touch the foot that is above the ground.

4. To paint feet, start with an "L" and develop the foot like this. Don't add too many feet for a crowd or they will look static.

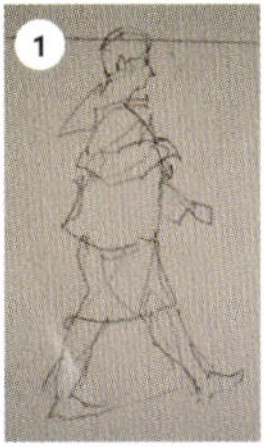

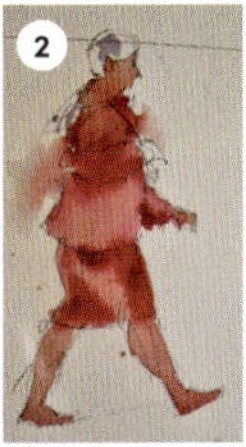

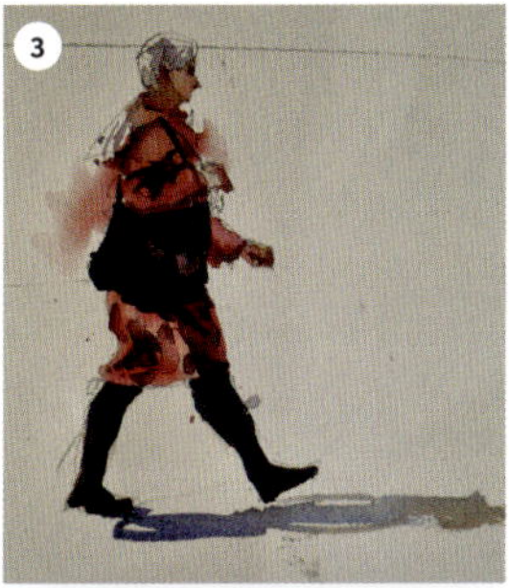

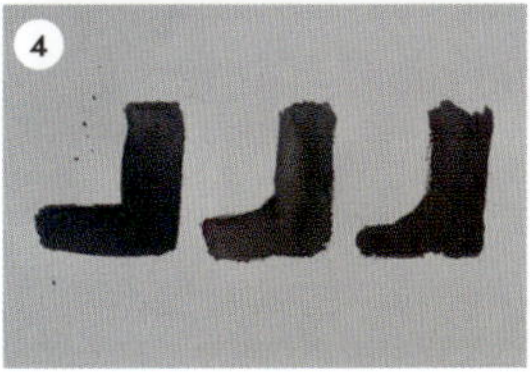

CHAPTER 9

Refine Your Painting

Finishing Touches

How do you finish a painting and how do you know when it's finished? These are hard decisions to make! It is tempting to keep adding another unnecessary mark, but equally those last touches of detail could bring the painting together. To me, a painting is finished when, to the best of my ability, I can't improve on it anymore. Here are some ideas on how to give your painting that extra polish.

When to Stop

Knowing when to stop is one of those hard calls in painting. A rule of thumb is if you are "fiddling," painting without a plan, then stop! It is better to leave something unsaid in a painting than give too much information. If you still feel your painting lacks something, here are some points to consider.

1. Go over the principles of design (see Chapter 5) and ask yourself if you have overlooked any of the points.

2. Stand at least five paces away or look at the painting in a mirror.

3. Put the painting away for a few days and then look at it again with a fresh eye.

4. Turn away from your painting and then look back. The first thing that you notice could be what the painting needs.

5. Ask someone else for their opinion. You can then accept or reject their ideas but try to justify that option.

Cropping

In my studio, I keep a mount board, cut diagonally in half. When I am assessing a painting for a better format, I place the mount in different positions on the painting to find a better composition. Cropping to a different format can completely change the focus. If a painting isn't working out, there may be a better way of presenting it by cropping part of the painting out.

When deciding whether to crop or not, keep in mind that, generally, the smaller the painting, the less detail you add. Larger paintings can take more detail. When cropping, remember to keep the focal point within the Golden Ratio.

Portrait format.

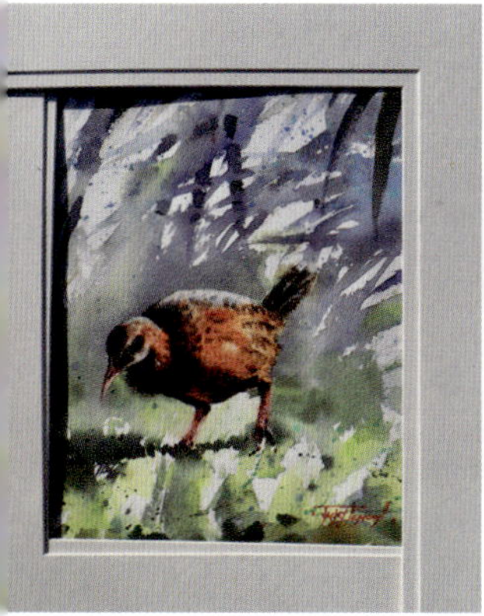

Landscape format.

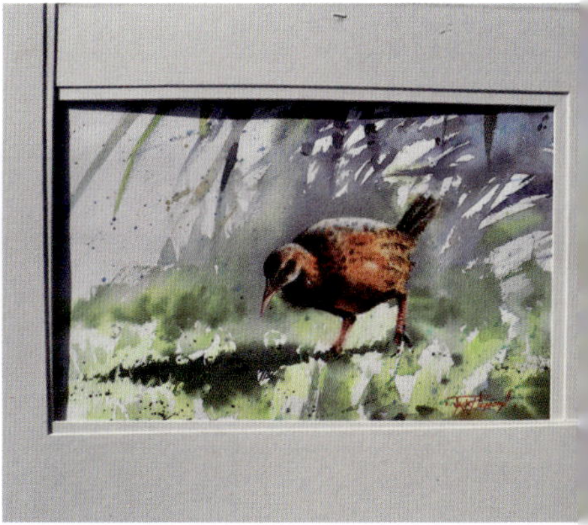

"New Zealand Weka" 2023, Langton Prestige.

Go to the Tap!

If you are a watercolor painter, you need to learn to swim! I have taught myself to wash back areas of a painting that just are not working well. I have no hesitation to "GO TO THE TAP"! and wash the offending area off. I turn on a tap in the bathroom, hold the painting under the running water, and gently swish this paint away with a large flat brush. Not all the paint will come off, there will be some staining. I protect the rest of the painting by holding it away from the water. However, some areas I am not targeting inevitably get wet so, afterwards, I lay the painting flat and place an old dish towel over the wet area, then gently press the dish towel while on the painting to soak up excess water. The paint is rarely disturbed, but it does takes a bit of practice, of course. I let the painting dry flat, and then repaint the area I washed off. Sometimes, I will repaint the area in before it has dried.

In this painting of Marcus (which won me a nice prize!), I felt that, compositionally, there was too much repetition of hair texture. I had the choice to start again or "go to the tap" for part of the hair. The blurry left side of his hair is where I water blasted under a strong outside tap by my studio! While at the damp stage, I painted the hair in again to give a softer texture and was really pleased with the result, as the hair is different on either side of his head. The focus is now on the screwed-up eyes as he is laughing, giving the painting more life to it.

"Marcus" 2024, Langton Prestige rough.

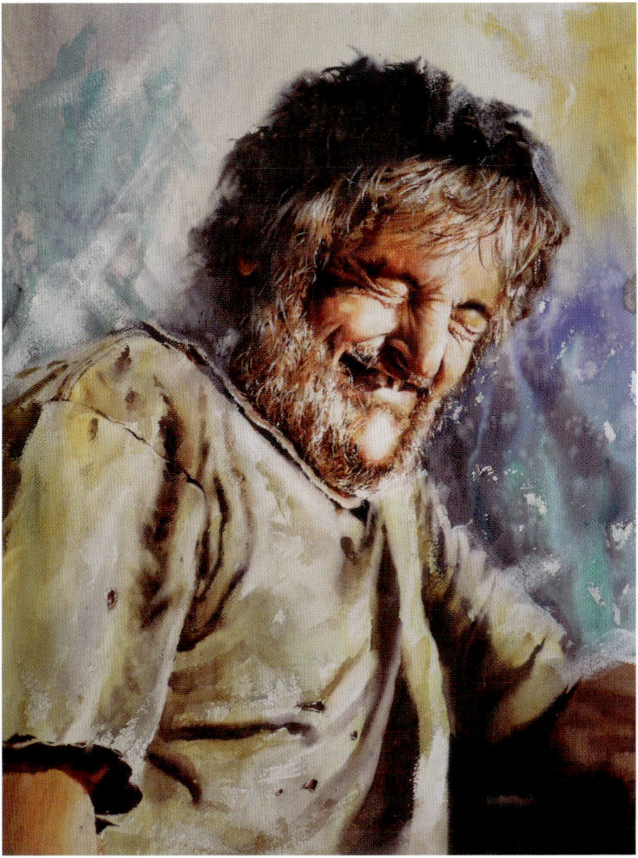

Trouble with Figures

A figure in the right spot in a landscape can be the perfect finishing detail to a painting that needs scale, motion, or a missing focal point. However, everyone, painter or not, is instinctively an expert on figure proportion, even when we are not! Sometimes, it takes me a few goes to get the figure looking just right. So, how can you correct a mistake?

DOUBLE PRIMING

If a figure isn't working and the rest of the painting is looking good, take it off by double priming:

1. Dry the painting.

2. Wet the paper over the figure you want to take out, leaving the water to soak in for a minute.

3. Rewet the area and with a stiff brush, gently scrub the figure out. Be careful not to damage the paper (100 percent cotton works best for this).

4. Dry the paper and paint the figure in again.

5. If there are still messy marks, I paint two figures in place of the one figure!

This technique is also suitable for small areas of your painting, but don't try it on large areas.

Splattering

Splattering water and paint is a great way to add movement into your painting. Hold the end of a synthetic round brush charged with a runny mix of paint (No. 1.5 mix). Protect areas that you don't want splattered with paper and bang on the ferrule of the brush with two fingers. Flicking water onto drying paint will create numerous small runbacks, which, in the right context, can add some innovative texture. On distant hills, this can give a lovely misty tree-clad effect.

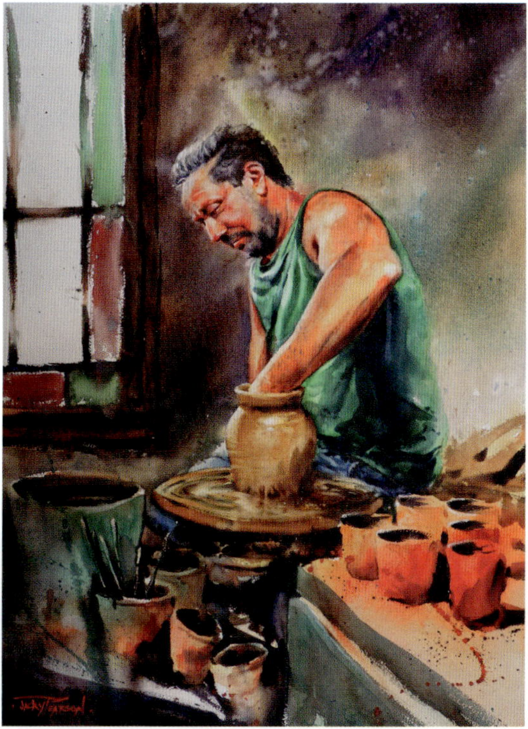

Here, I have splattered copious amounts of red and brown around on the lower part of the painting to give an extra sense of movement. While the paint was wet early on, I splattered water flicked from my fingers on the wall behind the potter. "The Potter" 2023, Langton Prestige rough.

Glazing

If you have a painting that lacks atmosphere, or a "certain something," try using the wet-on-dry glazing technique to change things up (see Chapter 4). You've got nothing to lose but everything to gain. Practice this on a "failed" painting first!

The purpose of glazing, a thin wash applied to dry paint, is to subtly change value or hue. It can be a series of many glazes, dried in between layers. Due to the transparency of the glaze, the eye sees other colors through the layers but they are subtly combined. I love bringing a dull painting to life with a new look.

WHITE GOUACHE GLAZING

I will often glaze with thin, white gouache. This glaze works well to set the background further away or create a lovely misty effect on a scene. Make sure your painting is very dry, so it is warm to touch with the back of your hand and not damp at all, front or back. Mix up a thin (No. 1.5) wash of white gouache and with a large flat brush, gently glide the wash over the area you want to glaze. It will look like thin milk but dry transparent and clear.

I felt the first painting **(1)** didn't have enough depth and atmosphere, so, using a large soft flat brush, I ran alternate thin (No. 1 mix) washes of Raw Sienna, Quinacridone Magenta, and Titanium White gouache over the dry sky and hills. I allowed each wash to dry thoroughly before adding another glaze. I don't always add this many glazes but I often glaze two or three times in the background of a painting **(2)**.

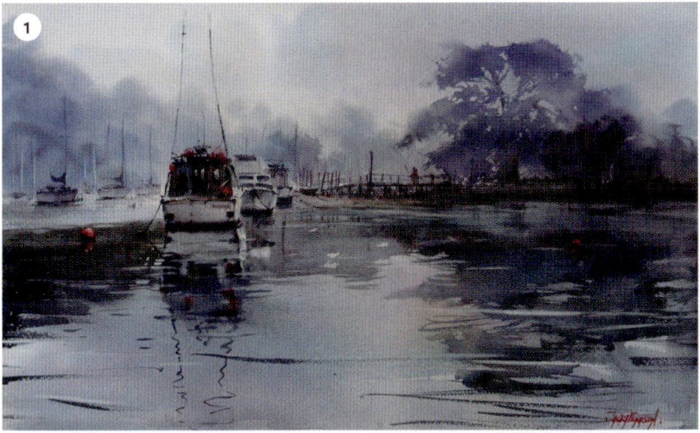

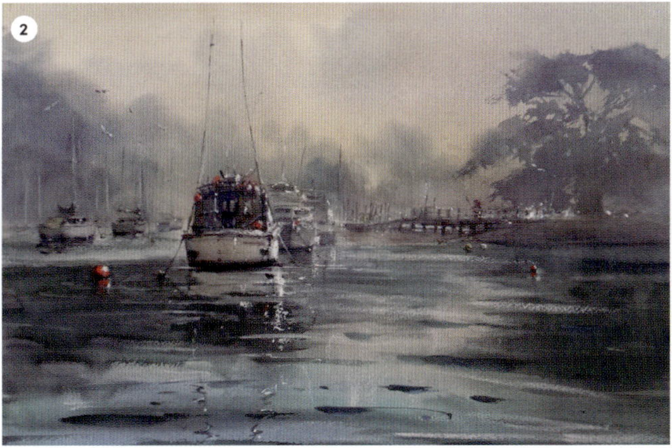

"Stillwater" 2018, Langton Prestige rough.

Other Marks

Here are some other tools and mark making that will add detail to your painting.

Be aware that, if your paper is not 100 percent cotton, it might not take too much sanding, rubbing, and rewetting. Test it out first on some scrap paper. A 100 percent cotton paper will take a lot of punishment!

Craft knife: use a craft knife to scrape dry paint off the paper to create highlights on water.

Sprinkling salt: while paint is wet, add salt and leave it to dry naturally, then rub the salt off the paper.

Soft pastel: adding a few white highlights with white pastel can look very effective.

Sandpaper: you can scratch out water sparkles with coarse sandpaper when paint is dry.

Credit card: make rocks by scraping through damp paint with the edge of a credit card. You can use the card to draw in grasses with vertical lines. When the paint is dry, you can add more shadows, and use the edge of the card to scratch into the paint for twigs and branches.

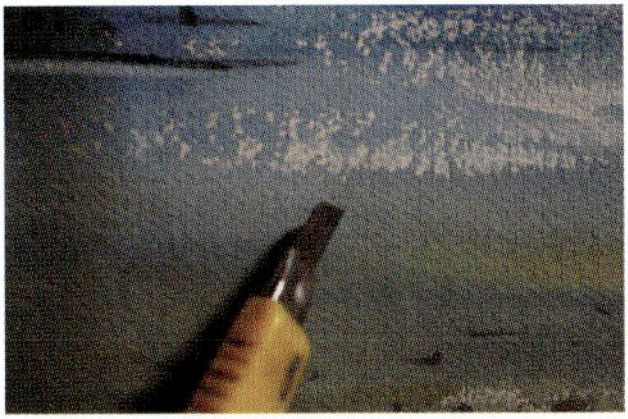

Using a craft knife.

Using salt to create texture.

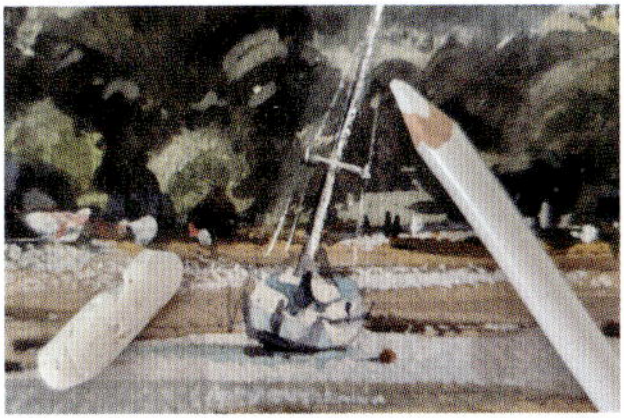

Using white pastel highlights.

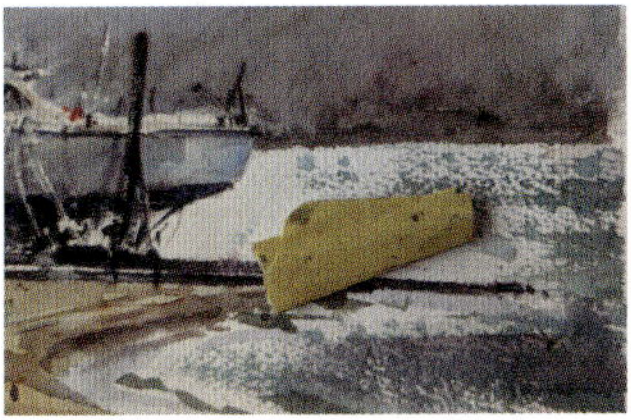

Using sandpaper to create sea spray.

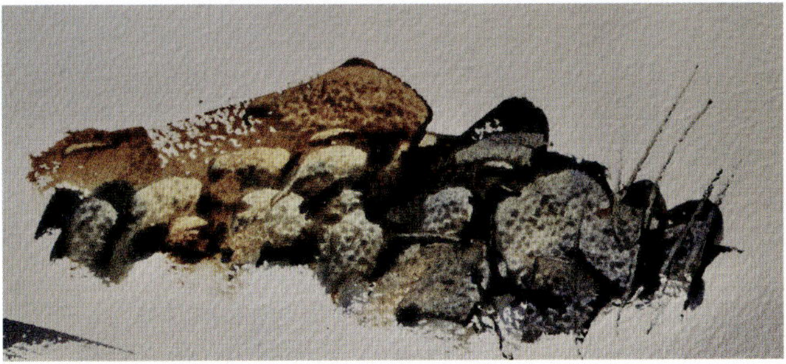

Rocks and grasses created with a credit card.

Save a Painting with Focal Points

Here's an idea for a sea or sky painting. Practice lots of birds on a scrap of paper. Then, choose the bird you like and place it in the Golden Ratio (see Balance in Chapter 5) area, as I've done here. Don't be tempted to put a few birds on the edge or right in the middle, as it doesn't look natural. A single gull will create movement and help with the story.

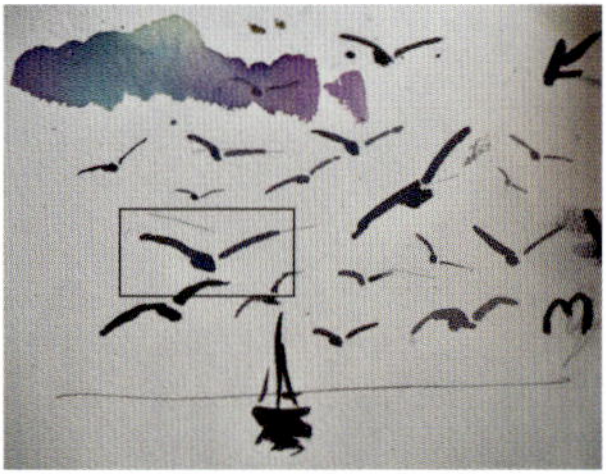

"Ahead of the Storm" 2020, Langton Prestige rough.

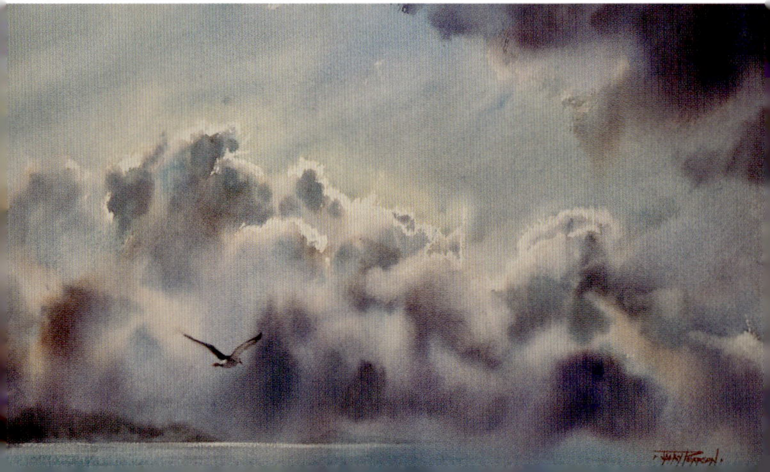

TRY THIS: STENCILING

This is a really useful way of adding in final elements to a painting, whether it's one that you are working on, or one that you want to improve. Cut out a variety of simple shapes (chickens, in this case) from thick paper with a craft knife. Place the stencil over the area you want to add the stencil to. Use a clean, damp synthetic flat brush to lift the paint and press the area clean with a tissue. Make sure there isn't too much water on your brush when lifting, otherwise it might leak under the stencil and make a messy shape. Remove the stencil and keep it to reuse in other paintings. When dry, add shadows and details to the stencil shape.

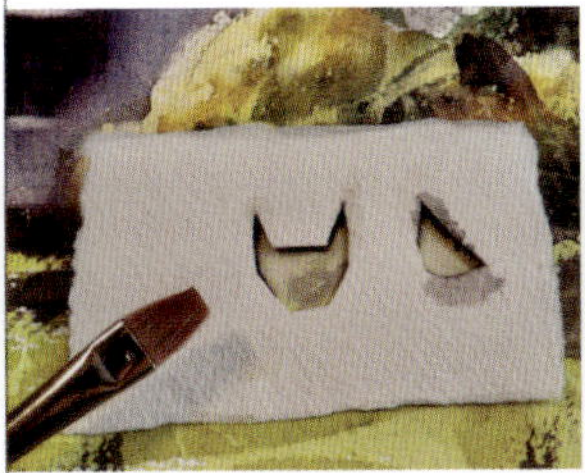

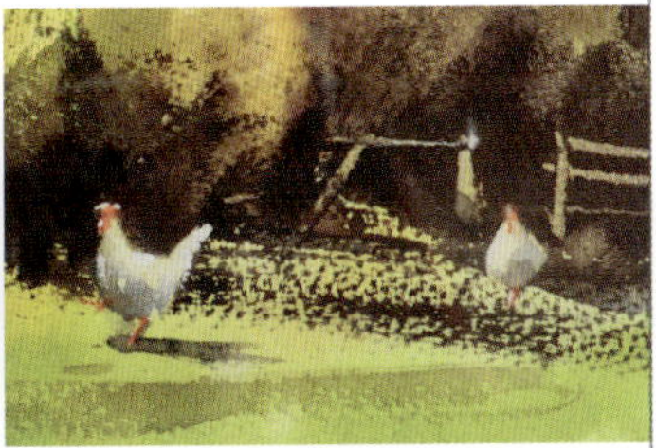

Stenciling out white chickens and then adding shadows and other details creates a fun but convincing way of producing light areas, without resorting to opaque white paint.

Your Signature

Only ever sign your work if it is your own original work from your own reference material, or unless you have permission from the owner of the reference.

Flattening Your Paper

Watercolor paper will always be flexing; it is the nature of the fibers as they absorb moisture from the atmosphere. You can improve any cockles in the paper with this method:

1. Your painting needs to be totally dry.

2. Turn your painting face down on some clean paper and board.

3. Wet the back of the paper but keep it a little away from the edges so water does not accidentally run underneath to the painting itself.

4. Add a clean board on top that is at least the size of the painting, ideally larger.

5. Add heavy weights, such as books, on top and leave for about 12 hours.

Keep a Record

It is a good idea to keep a photographic record of all your work and store it on a computer. Watercolors are very difficult to get a true image of due to the transparency of the paint. I take the photos in good light and put the painting flat on the floor so that I can stand over it evenly. I often use the grid on the camera. You can also take a photo of a framed painting through the glass with an app, such as PhotoScan (Google Photos), which will eliminate the glare.

Framing

Watercolor requires some form of protection because the paint will always be water soluble. Never put glass directly on top of your paper. It requires a mount board to separate it from the glass to avoid condensation disturbing the paint. Usually, a white or cream mount looks good without competing with the painting.

For longevity, use 100 percent cotton paper for the painting, which is acid free and protects your painting from strong light and foxing (brown age spots from acid leak). For UV protection, I very rarely use museum glass, which is horrendously expensive, and rely on using the best quality, lightfast pigments on the market. However, I do use conservation standard mounts and backing, which don't leak brown acids into the painting.

I am not keen on the matte look of anti-glare glass but it is an option if you have large windows and want to reduce the impact of glare.

If you're on a budget, homeware stores sell perfectly good inexpensive frames and you can recycle second-hand frames by repainting them.

A customer of this very large painting (5ft/1.5m in length framed, that's a lot of glass!), placed a light strip above the painting. This stops the glass glare very effectively.

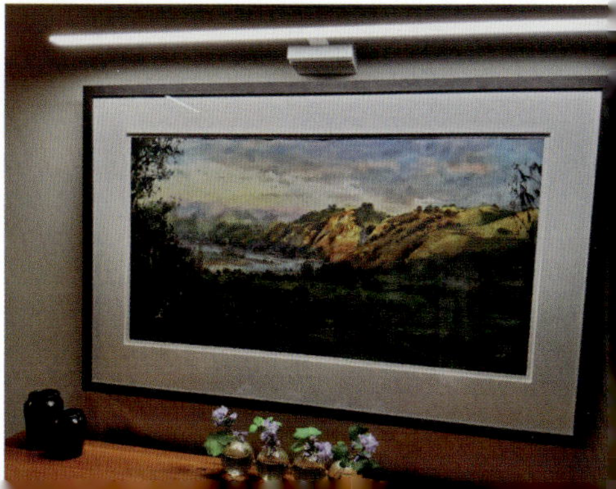

INDEX

About the Author

Jacky has been painting all her life and using watercolors professionally for 25 years. She now holds regular watercolor lessons and workshops in New Zealand and overseas, both in person and online. Jacky has been the recipient of many international and national awards and has been selected to represent New Zealand in international exhibitions. She often has artwork and articles published in international art magazines and books worldwide, such as the North American art books *Splash*. She has a successful worldwide calendar series, *Lighthouses of New Zealand*. Her painting demonstrations can be viewed on YouTube including Australian TV series "Colour in Your Life."

www.jackypearson.co.nz | @jackypearsonart.

Acknowledgments

Thank you Tony, for patiently waiting and being there for me while I fulfill my life's dream of being a full-time artist! Ann and Robin, Charles, Liggy Webb, Niall and Alice, for all the years they have advised me and taken me seriously.

Without a shadow of doubt, I owe so much to my lovely students, who over the years have supported and nurtured my painting life. Roy Aziz, who bought my first painting and encouraged me in my two careers! Eileen Kelly without whom I would not be teaching watercolor. Pam Darling for countless hours helping me pull my ideas together, and to Clare Ashton and the team at David and Charles Publishers.

A DAVID AND CHARLES BOOK

David and Charles is an imprint of
David and Charles, Ltd
Suite A, Tourism House, Pynes Hill,
Exeter, EX2 5WS

EU GPSR Authorized Representative:
Logos Europe, 9 rue Nicolas Poussin,
17000, La Rochelle, France
Email: Contact@logoseurope.eu

First published in the UK and USA in 2026

A catalogue record for this book is available from the British Library.

ISBN-13: 9781446317235 hardback
ISBN-13: 9781446317242 EPUB

This book has been printed on paper from approved suppliers and made from pulp from sustainable sources.

FSC www.fsc.org MIX Paper | Supporting responsible forestry FSC® C020056

Printed in China through Asia Pacific Offset for: David and Charles, Ltd, Suite A, Tourism House, Pynes Hill, Exeter, EX2 5WS

10 9 8 7 6 5 4 3 2 1

Publishing Director: Ame Verso
Senior Commissioning Editor: Nigel Browning
Publishing Manager: Jeni Chown
Editor: Victoria Allen
Copy Editor: Clare Ashton
Lead Designer: Sam Staddon
Designer: Anna Wade
Pre-press Designer: Susan Reansbury
Production Manager: Beverley Richardson

David and Charles publishes high-quality books on a wide range of subjects. For more information visit www.davidandcharles.com.

Share your art with us on social media using #dandcbooks and follow us on Facebook and Instagram by searching for @dandcbooks.

Layout of the digital edition of this book may vary depending on reader hardware and display settings.